MANAGEMENT
LOOKS AT
AFRICA

CONTRIBUTORS

Ludwig E. Armerding

Pierre Beurskens

Bernard Blankenheimer

J. C. Dean

Hamed Kamal Eldin

Saba Habachy

Roy B. Hill

Edmond C. Hutchinson

H. W. Manville

Richard Manville

C. J. Omana

Tore Rose

H. P. Van Aggelen

Forest G. Warren

EDITOR

Jerome W. Blood

MANAGEMENT

LOOKS AT

AFRICA

AMERICAN MANAGEMENT ASSOCIATION
NEW YORK

This book has been distributed without charge to AMA members enrolled in the International Management Division. Those members who are enrolled in other divisions, or who wish extra copies, may order the book in a hardcover edition at $6 per copy. Price to non-members, $9.

Library of Congress catalog card number: 66-24179

The last chapter of this book was prepared as a research report submitted in partial fulfillment of the requirements of Professor George C. Lodge at the Graduate School of Business Administration during the academic year 1965-1966. The report expresses only the conclusions and opinions of the author. It does not represent the views of the School or of any member of its faculty or staff, or of any business firm or individual contacted by the author.

FOREWORD

PERHAPS THE TITLE OF THIS BOOK should be "Management Looks at the *New* Africa"—for today's Africa is new and different from the continent as it was when most of us studied its geography. The change from colonial status under European control to independence with nationals of each new country in the command posts has created a new economic situation which offers major new opportunities to American businessmen.

Problems accompany the opportunities, as they always do, but many American businessmen have decided that the potential benefits make the risks worthwhile. Much of the material in this book consists of reports of some of these companies' actual experiences in Africa. We hope that this book will be of assistance in developing more and stronger commercial ties between the new Africa and the United States.

In addition, we are confident that even those managers whose companies may never do business in Africa can read this book with profit. The reason for this is that tremendous opportunities are opening up in all of the less developed regions of the world—Africa, Asia, and Latin America—and most of the management problems are of the very same type as those encountered in Africa by the companies represented in this book. Businessmen and managers from the developed areas must be aware of these opportunities and problems if the companies they represent are not to be left behind.

MILO MARSH
Manager
International Management Division

CONTENTS

OVERALL CHARACTERISTICS OF NORTH AFRICA AND THE MIDDLE EAST •

HAMED KAMAL ELDIN

IT IS REMARKABLE THAT THE COUNTRIES of North Africa have more in common with the Arab states of the Middle East than with the rest of Africa. Therefore, while the following survey will be primarily concerned with North Africa, it becomes meaningful to include these Middle Eastern states in order to have a reasonable understanding of the social, political, and economic conditions that influence the people who live in North Africa today.

Why are North Africa and the Middle East so important at present? First, this area occupies a particularly strategic position between two power alignments of states essentially opposing each other. Second, in an age which has come to depend in a very large measure on petroleum, the countries of the Middle East contain more than half of the world's petroleum reserves—this in addition to the vast reserves in the Algerian Sahara and the recently discovered enormous reserves in Libya. These two factors make the Middle East and North Africa an area whose attitudes and outlook may well exercise a decisive influence on the shape of things to come.

In an attempt to understand this area, let us have a look at its geography and population as well as its historical background.

HAMED KAMAL ELDIN is Systems Consultant with the Mobil International Oil Company, New York, New York. This material is based on presentations originally prepared by the author for AMA Briefing Sessions.

GENERAL INFORMATION

	Area (1,000 Sq. Miles)	Population (Millions)	Density (People per Sq. Mile)	Capital	Largest City	Main River
ALGERIA	920	11.60	13	Algiers	Algiers	Chéliff
MOROCCO	170	12.65	74	Rabat	Casablanca	Moulouya
TUNISIA	48	4.50	93	Tunis	Tunis	Medjerda
LIBYA	680	1.55	2	Bengazi & Tripoli	Tripoli	
EGYPT	386	28	72	Cairo	Cairo	Nile
U.S.A.	3,615	195	54			

TABLE 1

Geography. The area represents many physical contrasts. There are high and rugged mountains in Anatolia, Turkey, others fringing the great Iranian plateau, yet others fronting on the Mediterranean in Syria and Lebanon, and some in Morocco in North Africa. These are compensated for by predominantly low and flat expanses in Egypt, Arabia, and Mesopotamia. The rest consists mainly of wide expanses of desert or barren waste, uninhabited or occupied by nomadic or seminomadic tribes. This area, representing over four million square miles, is considerably bigger than the United States.

With respect to the principal features of the physical environment, about the only major generalization that will apply is that the area is *dry.* Over great portions there is insufficient precipitation to support any agricultural activities. Probably no other circumstance has exerted as much influence on the people who have moved into the area in the course of centuries as this single fact. It has shaped the culture now regarded as indigenous to the area. It has set rigid limits on the sizes of populations and determined their distribution. In this regard, it has brought about the situation in which countries with relatively small populations are sandwiched between two of the most populous parts of the earth—Europe and the subcontinent of India.

Table 1 gives general information for the states of North Africa. For each country it includes total area, total population, and density of population, as well as such other information as the capital, the largest city, and the main river. Corresponding U.S. information is included for comparison.

Population and social structure. What do the people of North Africa and the Middle East have in common? Are they all Arabs? Are they all Moslems? What about language?

The area can be divided into two groups of states—Arab and non-Arab —the latter comprising Turkey and Iran (and, of course, Israel, which is not included in this discussion). The Arab group of states represents over 80 million people while the non-Arab group represents over 50 million.

With the exception of Lebanon, which has a slight majority of Christians, Islam is the main religion in the whole area of North Africa and the Middle East. The Moslems represent 99 percent of the total population in Saudi Arabia and 98 percent in both Iran and Turkey, and the percentage is over 90 in the states of North Africa.

Arabic is the main language in the whole area of the Middle East and North Africa with the exception of Turkey, where they speak Turkish, and Iran, where the languages spoken are Persian and Kurdish. Arabic is the language of over 100 million people of the world. However, according to statistics over 500 million people are Moslems. It is important to note that Arabs are not necessarily Moslems. As a matter of fact, some of the strongest advocates of Arab unity are Arab Christians.

Although the population of the Arab world has the unity of Arabic language and Islamic religion, each region has developed an intimate local life with its own social structure, its special economic interests, and its particular relations with the outer world. Irrespective of this, however, the culture and language and religion of the Arabs still hold the field. Table 2 concerns specific social characteristics of the states of North Africa, with life span and literacy figures shown in comparison with those of the United

SOCIAL FACTORS

	Languages	Principal Religions	Life Span	Literacy
ALGERIA	Arabic French	Islam Christianity Judaism	48	15
MOROCCO	Arabic French Spanish	Islam	50	14
TUNISIA	Arabic French Italian	Islam	50	30
LIBYA	Arabic Italian	Isiam	49	30
EGYPT	Arabic	Islam Christianity	50	30
U.S.A.			70	98

TABLE 2

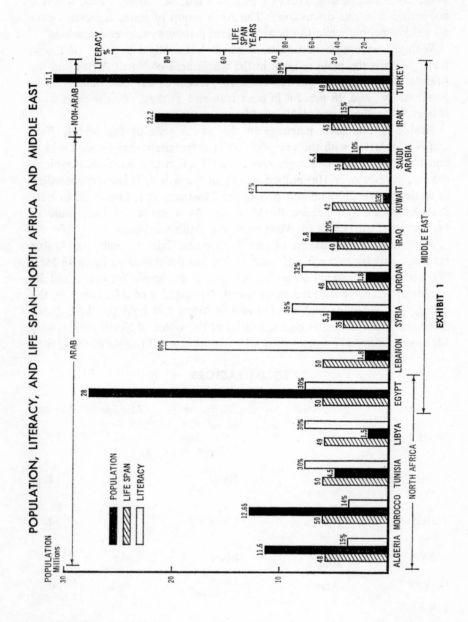

POPULATION, LITERACY, AND LIFE SPAN—NORTH AFRICA AND MIDDLE EAST

EXHIBIT 1

States. The graph in Exhibit 1 shows population, literacy, and life span for all the countries of North Africa and the Middle East. (Note that Egypt is considered a part of both regions.)

Historical background. The widest influence of Mohammed the Prophet (seventh century) and the first Arab Empire extended, at most, only to the inhabitants of the Arabian peninsula. Within a century after his death, the followers of Mohammed extended their rule and promoted their faith (Islam) throughout Mesopotamia, Syria, Palestine, Egypt, and the whole North African shore, as well as Spain. While these amazing conquests would have been impossible without the sense of unity and purpose provided by Islam, the invasion was essentially an expression of the Arab nation.

The middle of the eighth century marked the beginning of the dissolution of the Arab Empire. During the period that followed, and for several centuries, different dynasties assumed independent rulership. The political decline contributed to cultural stagnation.

The entire area was again brought together under Ottoman rule in the sixteenth century. While the Ottoman Empire established a nominal unity over the area, in fact it was as divided as ever. Separate countries, though theoretically under the Ottoman Empire, in practice enjoyed autonomy under independent rulers. For example, Egypt continued to be governed by Mamluk dynasties and later, in the early years of the nineteenth century, achieved autonomy under Mohammed Ali, an Albanian Turk. Morocco remained under the rule of the Alawite dynasty, and Algeria, Tunisia, and what is now Libya were ruled by various petty dynasties.

World War I brought the Ottoman Empire down to ruin. At the end of hostilities, little was left of it outside Anatolia in Asia and the environs of Constantinople in Europe.

Until the close of the eighteenth century the interests of Western Europeans—Venetians, French, and English—were confined to trade with the lands under Ottoman rule. Britain maintained friendly relations with the Ottoman rulers, extending both moral and military support. However, the French invasion of Egypt in 1798 brought the British to an awareness of the geographical importance of the Ottoman territories. Territorially, the beneficiaries of World War I in the Middle East and North Africa were Great Britain and France.

The treaty of Sèvres, in 1920, restored relations between the Allies— except the United States and Russia—and Turkey. It assigned Palestine, including Transjordan, and Mesopotamia (Iraq) to Britain as mandates

POLITICAL STATUS

	Government	Cold War Position	Important Historical Facts
ALGERIA	President; 1-house national assembly (1-party rule)	Nonaligned	Won freedom from France in 1962 after 7 years of war
MOROCCO	King and premier; 2-house parliament	Nonaligned	French and Spanish holdings combined as independent nation in 1956
TUNISIA	President; 1-house national assembly	Neutral (Favors West)	Formerly under French control; independence 1956
LIBYA	King and premier; 2-house parliament	Neutral (Favors West; U.S. and British bases)	Formerly Italian colony; independence 1951
EGYPT	President; 1-house national assembly (1-party rule)	Nonaligned	Formerly British protectorate; independence 1936

TABLE 3

ECONOMIC FACTORS

	Per-Person Output (Dollars)	GNP (Billions of Dollars)	Products	Trade Percent to U.S.A.	Percent from U.S.A.	Car	Phone	Radio	TV
ALGERIA	185	2.15	Livestock, grain, oil, fruit, vegetables, iron ore	0.6	7.0	60	75	12	77
MOROCCO	175	2.17	Phosphate, oil, manganese, grain, livestock, fruit	1.3	8.0	85	90	20	500
TUNISIA	185	0.85	Wheat, phosphate, iron ore, fruit, olive oil, livestock	11.0	9.5	90	140	11	830
LIBYA	360	0.60	Livestock, fruit, grain, peanuts, esparto grass, oil	8.6	25.4	55	130	8	260
EGYPT	140	4.00	Cotton, grain, oil, sugar, textiles, cement	7.0	27.0	330	105	9	67
U.S.A.	3,240	630				3	2	1	3

TABLE 4

or trust territories. Syria, including Lebanon, was entrusted to France, which also controlled most of North Africa.

World War II left the United States with little option of returning to a policy of isolation. Before 1945 the United States had looked upon the Middle East and North Africa as a sphere of European power, that of Britain in particular. The rise of U.S. interest somehow coincided with the decline of European influence in the area. It is only very recently that the competitive intervention of the Soviet Union has become apparent in the area.

The present century has been highlighted by independence of all the countries in the area. Egypt won her freedom from Britain in 1922—with reservations. The Anglo-Egyptian treaty of 1936 provided for the withdrawal of British troops from Egyptian territory except for the Suez Canal area. Withdrawal from this area took place in 1956.

Algeria had been considered as part of Metropolitan France. It won its freedom from France in 1962 after seven years of war. Tunisia, formerly under French control, achieved independence in 1956. In the same year Morocco was created as an independent nation, its territory combining the previous French and Spanish holdings. Libya, an Italian colony until the end of World War II and later under British and French military occupation, gained its independence in 1951.

Political climate. Political events have moved at a lively pace in recent years in most of the countries of the area. The predominance of the Islamic religion and the existence of a common language, Arabic, do not suggest political unity. The Arabs' gropings toward unity still are handicapped by factors that have influenced Arab development in the past and which continue to affect it today. The Arabs have traditionally been individualists, reluctant to accept authority except in moments of crisis and prone to rebel against it as soon as the crisis has passed. Oil and its revenues, instead of helping them to unite, have actually hindered Arab unification.

Also, there is the great ideological divide between the "socialist" and "capitalist" camps. Egypt with its wide-ranging state capitalism stands at one end of the spectrum. Saudi Arabia, a deeply conservative state, stands at the other. At various points in between are the states of Arab North Africa. Table 3 shows the political status of each North African country in terms of the kind of government it has and its position toward the two power alignments in the Cold War.

Economic development. All countries in the area now speak in earnest the language of five-year plans, development budgets, and production targets. However, of all the Arab states Egypt obviously belongs in a class of its own. A broad-based industrialization is the only possible road to prosperity for a country of such dense population and small area of cultivation. Before 1952 Egypt's industry was largely confined to the production of yarns and textiles. There were no basic iron and steel industries; cars, refrigerators, household appliances, and many other manufactured goods now produced or assembled in Egypt were almost wholly imported.

On completion of its five-year plan, Egypt should be nearing takeoff into self-sustained growth. There are problems, such as the rising consumption of the new urban working classes and the dire shortage of foreign currency. However, Egypt has been highly successful in securing loans and credits.

Compared with Egypt, the rest of the Arab countries are in many ways very fortunate. None of them has Egypt's high population. Iraq, Kuwait, Saudi Arabia, and lately Algeria and Libya have some of the most profitable oil fields in the world. Iraq and Syria have a rich agriculture potential. Lebanon thrives on commerce and services.

By and large, industry in these countries is limited to a few small oil refineries, textile production, food processing, and the manufacture of simple consumer goods. Most of these industries are largely the result of efforts exerted by private enterprise. However, the middle class as a driving force behind industrialization is not nearly so important in the Arab world as it is in the West. In all the Arab countries, both "socialist" and "capitalist," the governments are playing a key note in industrialization, because only the governments command the financial and other resources required for big projects.

Obviously, the Arab world shares many problems with underdeveloped countries in general. Most of the countries in the area have geared their industry mainly to agriculture. Indeed, socially and physically, industrialization will have a ruder impact on the Arab world than elsewhere.

With the exception of Kuwait, which set up a special fund for financing economically sound projects in the Arab world, there is a lack of economic coordination among the Arab states. They do very little trade with each other. The Arab common market is an experiment that every Arab watches with every wish for success.

Table 4 gives some economic information pertinent to the North African states. The data include main products, trade with the United States, and number of people sharing a car, phone, radio, or TV, whether or not this information can be considered as a true measure of the standard of living. The U.S. figures are again included for comparison. Note also that the

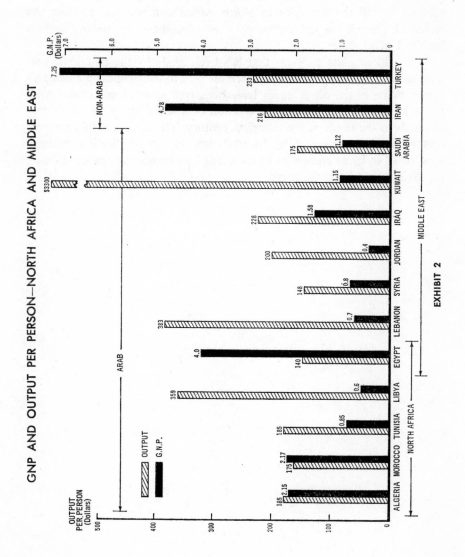

GNP AND OUTPUT PER PERSON—NORTH AFRICA AND MIDDLE EAST

EXHIBIT 2

average output per person in North Africa is $200 as compared with less than $100 for the rest of Africa.

Exhibit 2 is a chart showing the output per person and the gross national product for all the countries in North Africa and the Middle East. As indicated, Kuwait has the highest per-capita income in the world—including the United States.

In considering the progress that has been made by these nations, perhaps the disappointments are too often allowed to overshadow the achievements. Some of the oil revenues have been well spent. Some of the Arab rulers have taken the lead in the erection of a social structure which corresponds to the needs of the twentieth century. The change within the past century has been tremendous. In education, in industrialization, perhaps most of all in its awareness of its own social problems and responsibilities, the Arab world is on the move.

ECONOMIC AND LEGAL
PROBLEMS OF INVESTMENT
IN SUB-SAHARA AFRICA •

With Special Reference to Ethiopia and Nigeria

SABA HABACHY

THE ARABIAN NIGHTS is one of the great works of world literature. Everyone is familiar with the adventures of Sindbad the Sailor. According to the story of one of his seven voyages, he was shipwrecked but finally swam to safety on an uncharted island. He did not know what sort of people inhabited the island. Were they backward? Unfriendly? Or decent human beings? Suddenly he saw the islanders coming out to meet him on the beach with soldiers in armor. He thought this was the end of him. But, contrary to his dim forebodings, he was taken to the capital of the island with pomp and ceremony and crowned king. He discovered that it was the custom of his newly found subjects, when their king died, to go to the beach, lay hands on the first man shipwrecked on their shores, and make him king.

Traveling frequently to Africa and, more specifically, to Ethiopia and Nigeria, I have asked myself the question: Why are Americans, usually thought of as pioneers and risk takers, at the bottom of the list in ventures in sub-Sahara Africa? Why do the British and the French invest in Africa

---

SABA HABACHY is Consultant, Arabian American Oil Co., New York, New York. This chapter was prepared shortly before the recent *coup d'état* in Nigeria. Government officials referred to in the text were those in office at the time. The author points out that, while some of these individuals have changed, the policies of Nigeria have not.

19

while American enterprise in that continent is hardly beginning to be felt? American enterprise and capital are certainly no less daring than their British or European counterparts, but American entrepreneurial ability avoids Africa because it is far away and not adequately known. Entrepreneurs in this country are more familiar with conditions in Canada and South America, to which the greater part of American investments go. Being insufficiently informed about Africa, they are reluctant to tread on what is for them uncharted ground. It is in man's nature to be afraid of the unknown, just like Sindbad when he swam to the island fearing for his life only to find a kingdom instead.

The popular saying is true: "The devil you know is preferable to the devil you do not know." Substitute "risk" for "devil" and you have the reason for the fact that the flow of American capital to Africa south of the Sahara is only a trickle. However, with the fast and easy communication afforded by direct airlines to African capitals, the excuse of remoteness is no longer valid. Sub-Sahara Africa has become as much at America's doorstep as Canada, South America, Western Europe, or Japan.

NO SUBSTITUTE FOR PERSONAL KNOWLEDGE AND EXPERIENCE

The discovery of Africa started in the second half of the nineteenth century. Thanks to the Stanleys and Livingstones, we are now familiar with the geographical features of the so-called Dark Continent, the sources of its mighty rivers, its high mountains, and its vast lakes.

Today, after more than a hundred years, we are still in the process of discovering the Dark Continent, but the emphasis has shifted to natural resources, economic opportunities, and investment. Here we have barely scratched the surface. We are familiar with Africa's potential for hydroelectric power. Dams have been built or planned. Today the Kariba Dam on the Zambesi and the High Dam on the Nile are very much in the news. Surveys have pointed out that African rivers and lakes represent two-fifths of the world potential for hydroelectric power. In mineral wealth and primary products, Africa has been aptly described as a storehouse of raw materials for the rest of the world. In a large measure, the West depends on Africa for cocoa, sisal, and oil seeds and for a long list of minerals which includes uranium, industrial diamonds, copper, manganese, cobalt, beryl, asbestos, chrome, zinc, and lead. The emerging countries of Africa also provide an increasingly expanding market for manufactured goods of all kinds. Finally, there is in Africa a substantial reserve of manpower to draw upon.

The West, also, can now count on the cooperation of Africans and the emerging African states. They are proud of their newly won independence and anxious to follow the caravan of economic progress. What can the West offer, in return, to satisfy Africa's urgent needs? The answer is investment of capital, science, and modern technology. This country spends annually more than $17 billion on research, some of which is of real significance for Africa. But Africa needs its institutions, its legal systems, and its economic setup to be better known in the West.

Here is a good example of what can be done in this respect: studies are being carried out under fellowships granted by the American Society of International Law in its research program on foreign investment and economic development. For instance, the studies of Paul O. Proehl, professor of law at the University of California in Los Angeles, have resulted in an excellent book.[1] And, writing about a country on the other side of the African continent, Dean Paul of the Law School of Haile Selassie University in Addis Ababa, together with a group of American and Swiss professors, is better acquainting us with Ethiopian legal institutions. We need more of this sort of effort, which should be extended to cover the Sudan, the Cameroons, and Zambia.

But nothing can replace personal study of legal and economic conditions on the spot. On the basis of visits to Nigeria and Ethiopia, I would rate the opportunities and climate for investment in sub-Sahara Africa as quite good, especially in the two countries named. I shall, in fact, focus attention throughout this discussion on these countries—which, to be sure, I offer as mere illustrations. Conditions in many other African countries are more or less similar.

We should not, however, be carried away by the encouraging signs and the growing incentives to Western investment. We must also be mindful of the existence of some handicaps. It is true that public funds from national and international sources have been forthcoming in building up the essential economic infrastructure of emerging countries in Africa. Nigeria and Ethiopia are among the principal beneficiaries of loans and other aid from such international institutions as the World Bank, the International Finance Corporation, and the United Nations Special Fund. They have also received foreign aid in different forms directly from Western governments and are earmarking substantial amounts of their gross national income for the building of roads, communications systems, dams, and public utilities. These expenditures create favorable conditions for private initiative and investment. There is, however, a lag between the public and private sectors of the economy. Individual enterprise is still far from

[1] *Foreign Enterprise in Nigeria,* University of North Carolina Press, 1965.

having realized the development potential and propitious conditions which have been created. Much remains to be done in this respect to the mutual advantage of both foreign investors and host countries, but it must also be said that the entrepreneur should not be carried away by African expectations, which may well, at times, run ahead of available resources.

A BALANCE SHEET: THE PLUSSES AND THE INCENTIVES

Let us try to determine the factors favorable to foreign investment which might be noted on the right-hand side of the ledger. We shall be concentrating, remember, on Nigeria and Ethiopia as the two outstanding countries in sub-Sahara Africa in this respect.

First and foremost, Nigeria has *a highly developed and effective legal system*. This is one of the best features of the legacy which Great Britain has bequeathed to Nigeria. The Supreme Court justices of the Federal Government and of the governments of the four regions of Nigeria have shown independence and legal learning under the most trying political circumstances. The Nigerian judiciary, educated in British and Nigerian universities in the excellent tradition of the common law, counts many outstanding jurists. In their hands, private property is secure, contracts are binding on both the governors and the governed, and acquired rights are respected.

Several Nigerian jurists have attained international prominence. For example, Federal Chief Justice Sir Adetokundo Amendola is noteworthy for his role in the World Rule of Law movement and in sponsoring and formulating the "Law of Lagos," a basic statement of law made under the auspices of the International Commission of Jurists. Another figure of importance in national and international law is Sir Louis Mbanefo, chief justice of Eastern Nigeria, who has served on the International Court of Justice as an *ad hoc* judge in the South-West Africa cases. The former premier of the northern region made this very relevant and significant statement in the Parliament of Northern Nigeria on the rule of law and its role in providing security for private foreign investment:

> Honorable members will appreciate that our future prosperity as a Region will depend largely upon the confidence which the world at large places in the probity of our institutions and especially the courts and the system of law which they administer. If there is lack of confidence, the result will inevitably be that we shall not obtain the foreign capital and investment which we need in order to expand our economy and develop our social services.

The same points can be made about Ethiopia—with this difference, however: the Fascist government under Mussolini systematically deprived Ethiopia of its intelligentsia. Consequently, the Government of His Majesty the Emperor had the good sense to use expatriate judges temporarily until such time as an intellectual élite could be educated in a modern legal tradition. Ethiopia forgave and forgot. Many Italian jurists still practice law there, especially in Eritrea. Ethiopian students have been sent to law schools in this country, in Canada (especially to McGill University), and in Great Britain and France. His Majesty gave Ethiopia up-to-date modern codes. The Civil Code has been written by Professor René David, of the University of Paris; the Penal Code is the work of Professor Graven, former dean of the Law School of the University of Geneva, whose son now sits on the Supreme Court of Ethiopia. As is the case in Nigeria, English is an official language used before the courts.

The teaching of law in Ethiopia is carried on under the Sailer project, financed by a grant from the Ford Foundation. A remarkable feature of this instruction is the popularity of the night courses in law and public administration organized by Dean Paul, an American, for high Government officials. In 1965, an alumni association was formed in Addis Ababa, and a member of the Ethiopian Parliament was elected president. He had followed the night courses and familiarized himself with modern legal techniques and procedures. The first group of regular day students was graduated in January of that year.

Second, because of sound planning, both Nigeria and Ethiopia have *a favorable climate for investment and propitious economic conditions.* May I quote from Professor Proehl's recent book about Nigeria, in which he says:

> Nigeria is showing constant increases in gross national product. A six-year economic development plan was put into effect in 1962. This calls for a total of new investments in productive assets and facilities... [amounting to] 1.1 billion pounds sterling. Of this, 549 million is to come from domestic savings, both public and private—the difference between national income and consumption. It is hoped that 327 million pounds sterling will be provided by foreign governments and international agencies in loans and grants. The United States has already pledged 80 million pounds sterling. . . . Finally, private investors are expected to bring 200 million pounds sterling. While domestic private investments have been sustained, foreign private investment has not lived up to expectations. The lag of foreign investments since independence is attributable to a number of factors: a "wait-and-see" attitude on the part of foreign investors after Nigeria struck off on its own; and a lack of knowledge and interest on the part of foreign investors.[2]

[2] *Op. cit.*

In his keynote speech opening the last elections, Dr. Michael Okparra, the former premier of Eastern Nigeria, stated: "Unfortunately we have found that American interest in the industrialization of Nigeria is slow and tardy."

Turning now to Ethiopia, we find similar economic planning and an equally healthy and hospitable climate for foreign investment. We also find the same disappointment at the slowness and tardiness of foreign investors in realizing the rewarding opportunities open to them. The need for foreign private capital is even greater in Ethiopia than it is in Nigeria, although there is, to be sure, some difference between the two countries in population, extent of territory, and natural resources.

Nigeria has a dense population of over 50 million inhabitants. Its resources are varied: agricultural, mineral, and hydroelectric. A great dam is planned on the river Niger. Oil has been discovered in Eastern and Midwestern Nigeria and will soon become the most important commodity produced for local consumption as well as for export. Last, but not least, Nigeria provides the largest mass market in Africa where limited-scale mass production can be economically escalated as the needs of its inhabitants rise. To this must be added the fact that as Africa moves to create a common market, Nigeria may serve as the natural industrial center from which goods will flow to West Africa.

By contrast, Ethiopian industry can count on satisfying only the needs of the local market of 15 to 20 million inhabitants. Its agricultural potential, however, is the highest in Africa. Hydroelectric power is in process of being developed, but rather slowly. Exploration for oil is going on, especially offshore in the Red Sea. There is a wealth of research on Ethiopia's natural resources and on the economic opportunities it offers to investors. Most of this research is due to substantial financial and technical aid from the United States. However, as in Nigeria, private initiative on the part of U.S. investors lags behind. Hitherto they have done little in translating this research into action and concrete realization. Much of it is still buried in files from which it has to be dug out. There is on the part of prospective U.S. investors in Ethiopia the same attitude of wait-and-see which we have encountered in Nigeria. In both countries, the British have done and are doing a better job. In connection with the U.S. funds which have been spent on scientific research in Ethiopia, one is reminded of the ancient Egyptian money changers who uselessly hoarded their treasures under the walls of the Temple of Karnak and forgot about them until Egyptologists discovered them after some three thousand years.

Let me give some examples of this valuable American research work in Ethiopia:

- The United States has provided the funds and the scientists for a thorough survey of the basin of Lake Tana and the Blue Nile.
- The meat resources of Ethiopia are vast. The number of cattle alone —not to speak of sheep and goats—is estimated at 27 million. Veterinary services and inoculation against animal diseases are provided by American financial and technical aid. Yet this food potential is barely beginning to be utilized, and not by American enterprise but by British and Israeli interests. The well-known British firm of Mitchell Cotts has recently entered into a partnership with the Ethiopian Government to do meat processing and packaging.
- In the field of agriculture, three-quarters of Ethiopia's 450 thousand square miles is fertile soil which can grow anything. Herodotus, the father of history, describes Egypt as "a gift of the Nile." More accurately, it is the gift of Ethiopia and the Blue Nile, which has eroded and carried away some of the fertile volcanic soil of that country to form the Nile Valley. Yet, in Ethiopia itself, barely 2 percent of this fabulous virgin soil, estimated at a hundred times the extent of Egypt's agricultural land, is rationally cultivated. The United States has provided the funds which made it possible for an American university to give Ethiopia an excellent school of agriculture; but, out of the first group of 26 Ethiopian graduates, only two were able to use their knowledge in agricultural pursuits. Because of their failure to raise the modest capital needed to buy seed and machinery, the remaining 24 have gravitated into clerical jobs in Addis Ababa. One of them complains that all that he did last year was write two routine letters. What a waste of valuable human resources!

The basic advantage which agricultural and industrial investments in virgin Africa have over the economies of developed countries can be briefly stated. While a return of 6 to 8 percent is considered good in the United States, Canada, Britain, South America, and Europe, I would estimate the rate of profitability in agricultural and industrial investments in Nigeria and Ethiopia conservatively at an average of 15 to 20 percent. Annual interest rates of 20 percent on loans are not uncommon in both countries. Naturally, part of this greater profitability is in the nature of an insurance premium against the greater risks facing venture capital in a developing country. Still, this leaves a substantial margin of profit from investments in pioneering enterprise in sub-Sahara Africa.

The third advantage on the right-hand side of the balance sheet consists of *the incentives provided by law*. In Nigeria these incentives take the form of pioneer-industry status attested to by the issuance of a pioneer certificate. This entitles the entrepreneur to a tax holiday of five years, favorable write-offs of capital equipment, and tariff protection, if he needs it, to ward off competition from imports while his business is still in its infancy. Capital may be forthcoming from the newly established Nigerian Development Bank. The Government will assist in securing land for factories. Planned areas that are close to shipping facilities and markets, with already constructed roads and necessary utilities, have been developed near several cities. Apart from relief from income tax, the accelerated rate of depreciation constitutes an appreciable incentive. To the normal rate of depreciation of from 5 to 15 percent for machinery and equipment and 20 percent for industrial buildings there is added an accelerated depreciation rate of 40 percent for the write-off of machinery. Depreciation allowances may be deferred until the end of the tax holiday when they may be claimed in full. If taxable income is less than the capital allowances claimed, the unabsorbed balance may be carried forward indefinitely. Losses may also be carried forward for as many as 10 years against future taxable profits.

The incentives to investors provided in the Ethiopian Investment Decree of 1963 are practically the same: a tax holiday of five years from commencement of production, the duty-free importation of machinery and equipment, guaranteed convertibility of dividends, and the repatriation of foreign capital in the currency of its country of origin. However, Ethiopia does not limit these incentives to a pioneer industry. Any new industry which is considered by the Ethiopian Investment Commission to be helpful to the national economy qualifies for them. Loans from the Development Bank of Ethiopia may be arranged, and the participation of the Development Bank in the equity also is a possibility. All these facilities can be negotiated in advance, and a letter of intention may be obtained from the Investment Commission pledging the incentives provided in the decree. Furthermore, the minister of finance has discretionary powers to grant additional relief from public charges such as excise and other duties, and the Government will give favorable consideration to requests for changes in the structure of customs duties in order to foster new industries.

I should like to stress one important point: these incentives are taken seriously by the two countries. In the case of two industrial projects with which I happen to be familiar in Nigeria and Ethiopia, I can testify that the law was smoothly and satisfactorily applied and that the promised advantages were forthcoming with some delay but without any difficulty. I have no doubt that foreign investments are welcomed in Nigeria and Ethiopia, in both word and deed.

Finally, I attach special importance to *the protection of industrial property*—patent rights, industrial designs, trademarks, and copyrights. This is because I believe that there is a chance to invest these intangible assets with little cost or sacrifice in sub-Sahara Africa under the existing forms of licensing agreements. Without entering into legal details, it would be correct to say that these valuable intangible rights are sufficiently protected. As a concrete example, the U.S. soft drink industry in Nigeria and Ethiopia is satisfied that trademarks covering its products are not in danger of infringement. Nor, it can be said, are patent rights and technical processes which cover some of the results of highly specialized scientific research used in oil exploration in both Nigeria and Ethiopia.

Nigeria is a party to two multilateral conventions relating to the protection of intangible property. These are the International Convention for the Protection of Industrial Property and the Universal Copyright Convention. Under the United Kingdom Registration Ordinance of 1925, patents granted in that country may be registered in Nigeria within three years of such grant with the Nigerian registrar of patents through an agent in Nigeria authorized to accept service of process for the grantee. Once granted, the Nigerian patent, aside from extending the patent right to Nigeria, becomes coextensive with that in the United Kingdom. It relates back to the date of the grant there and continues in force only as long as it remains valid in the United Kingdom. If it is renewed, submission of the British certificate of renewal to the registrar in Nigeria will similarly extend the life of the patent there. The same applies to an order of a court of competent jurisdiction extending the period of validity of the patent.

There is as yet no provision for the regulation of designs in Nigeria. However, protection is afforded if the design has been registered in the United Kingdom under the Patents and Designs Act. As for trademarks, they are satisfactorily protected by the comprehensive ordinance of 1955, which is the present law governing this matter in Nigeria.

Perhaps some concrete facts will give an idea of the success with which these laws operate. There has been a dramatic increase of registered trademarks in Nigeria, from 3,000 in 1961 to over 13,000 in 1963. (It must be noted that the majority of these trademarks are foreign.) These figures are indicative, also, of the fast tempo of business development and industrial growth.

The law protecting intangible rights and industrial property in Ethiopia has not reached a similar stage of development. Patent and trademark laws are being written at the present time, and administrative machinery for registration is contemplated. Meanwhile, under the Civil and Commercial Codes of Ethiopia there is ample protection for these rights under the principles of equity. Lack of public registry is made up for by publication in the daily papers which, together with continued use, creates a presumption of ownership.

The incorporation of a limited liability company in Nigeria is easy and satisfactory. Nigeria follows the pattern of the United Kingdom Company Act of 1948. Similarly, the creation of a public share company in Ethiopia under the Civil and Commercial Codes of 1960 presents no difficulties. However, lawyers' fees in Nigeria are quite high—practically comparable to fees in the United States—although the equivalent fees are much less in Ethiopia. Legal talent in both countries is far short of the need. There are 1,600 lawyers in Nigeria, and the number is much less in Ethiopia in comparison with the population.

It is hardly necessary to mention the favorable industrial factors which sub-Sahara Africa shares in common with other underdeveloped areas of the world: availability of raw materials and savings on the cost of labor, for example.

THE MINUSES AND THE DISINCENTIVES

Despite the great economic potential and the encouraging trend of economic development in sub-Sahara Africa, the picture is far from being all bright. There are some handicaps and deterrents too. To be objective, the following items should be entered on the liabilities side of the balance sheet I am presenting. They are common to both Nigeria and Ethiopia.

The first handicap to be overcome is nonpolitical. Businessmen rightly consider *the procrastination and the routine of a slow-moving bureaucracy* as the most serious obstacle to investment. Until a short time ago, visas to Nigeria and Ethiopia were hard to come by. When a visa was finally issued, it was often restricted to too short a stay to make an adequate survey. In both Nigeria and Ethiopia, approval of pioneer-industry status may drag on interminably. Files are lost or misplaced, and the same application has to be presented more than once. On my last trip to Nigeria, I brought to the attention of the authorities a request for relief from an unjustified excise tax. That request had been presented by Nigerian Textile Mills many months before. I was asked to present a new request or a copy of the former one. In Ethiopia, it took the better part of a year to negotiate a loan with the Development Bank and to get a letter of intention from the Investment Commission for a new industry to qualify for the incentives provided in the investment decree.

Such delays add to the cost of the projected enterprise and work to the disadvantage of both the foreign investor and the host country. Furthermore, they create a feeling of frustration and impatience. After a stay of ten years in a sub-Sahara country, and after rendering much unpaid service, a foreigner described it as one in which you lose patience if you have any and learn patience if you have none. However, this state of affairs is understandable in a country where there is a scarcity of competent personnel ready to take its responsibilities seriously. It takes time to train the officials necessary to run efficient and effective administrative machinery. Of late, however, conditions in this respect happily have been improving.

The former prime minister of Eastern Nigeria once addressed a select group of American industrialists and businessmen at a meeting especially arranged for him at the headquarters of the Chase Manhattan Bank in New York. He pleaded for investments in his region, which has now become the richest in Nigeria owing to the discovery of oil. At question time, one American investor in a textile mill brought to the attention of the prime minister the fact that it had been six months since his company had requested entry visas for a number of expatriate technicians and that he was still waiting for an answer. "I will fix that immediately," said the prime minister, and he did. Instructions have now been given to Nigerian consulates to facilitate and expedite the issue of visas.

As for the situation in Ethiopia, visas formerly were difficult to obtain from the only Ethiopian consulate in the United States—Washington—to which the applicant had to travel in person. At the present time, however, visas good for 30 days are automatically given at the airports of Addis Ababa and Asmara on arrival, and the 30-day period can be extended on request.

Where foreign experts are to be admitted, it will be advisable for the would-be investor to indicate, in presenting his project, the number of expatriate technicians which will be needed. This applies to both Nigeria and Ethiopia. In the textile industry, it was very much appreciated in both countries that the two textile mills with which I am connected established a school to train Nigerian and Ethiopian nationals. In the case of Ethiopian Fabrics Share Company, one of the features of the project which proved most attractive to authorities was the sending of six Ethiopian students to the manufacturers of machinery in Europe for training and experience in the use of the equipment. These skilled workers are now back in Asmara, where they have been of invaluable assistance in the assembly of the machinery. I might add that we had little difficulty in getting the necessary residence permits for the foreign technicians.

The second handicap which deters prospective investors is *fear of nationalization,* or insistence on premature and hasty Nigerianization or Ethiopianization. It is my considered opinion that this fear is exaggerated. In the case of Nigeria and Ethiopia it does not exist now and should not materialize for a long time to come. This is due to two simple facts. The first is that foreign capital is badly needed in both countries and will continue to be needed for the foreseeable future. And, second, there is very little as yet to nationalize or expropriate, and it stands to reason that local authorities, whatever social philosophy they may espouse, do realize that it is not worth their while to nationalize or expropriate so little and thereby stop the flow of future investments. Once there was an attempted *coup d'état* in Ethiopia during the absence of His Majesty the Emperor on a visit to Brazil. There were some markedly so-called progressive tendencies on the part of the revolutionaries. However, a noteworthy feature of the insurrection was the fact that no foreigner was harmed and no foreign property was touched by either of the warring factions.

One of the former leaders of Nigeria's Eastern Region professes "socialist" tendencies. However, words and slogans have different meanings in Africa from those ascribed to them in the West. Political leaders of sub-Sahara developing countries have defined their "socialism" as being neither Eastern nor Western but African. The influence of Chinese and Russian communism in Africa is now suffering serious setbacks. It is hardly noticeable in Ethiopia. In Nigeria, the former prime minister of the Eastern Region, Dr. Michael Okpara, had this to say about his concept of socialism:

> How can a government manufacture cement plants, iron and steel, locomotives, everything on earth? It could be done, but we do not think we will do it as rapidly as if we restricted government activities to a few specific fields as we have done in our country—electricity, the railways, the ports, coal, iron and steel, life insurance. That is just about all, and then the rest is an open field for the enterprising industrialist from any part of the world.

Such "mixed economy" conditions are no different from those prevailing in France, for example, where enterprise is about equally divided between the public and private sectors.

A fact which may give additional comfort to prospective American investors in Nigeria and Ethiopia is that both countries are cosignatories with the United States of a treaty which guarantees U.S. investments against nationalization without compensation upon the condition that the host state approve the enterprise beforehand. The host state, under these provisions, recognizes the subrogation of the U.S. Government to the claims of the American investors, who would receive compensation directly from the U.S. Government, leaving the more problematic function of collecting from the host country to the State Department.

American investors in sub-Sahara Africa may receive comfort from another direction—that is, some recent developments in international law. I am referring to the 1962 Resolution No. 1803 (XVII) of the General Assembly of the United Nations on permanent sovereignty over natural resources. That resolution reads as follows:

> Nationalization, expropriation or requisitioning shall be based on grounds or reasons of public utility, security or national interest which are recognized as overriding purely individual or private interests, both domestic and foreign. In such cases the owner shall be paid appropriate compensation, in accordance with the rules in force in the state taking such measures in the exercise of its sovereignty and in accordance with international law.

Here again, Nigeria and Ethiopia were among the 88 nations that approved the resolution—to observe agreements to arbitrate and to adhere to principles of international law. However, this adherence on the part of Nigeria and Ethiopia merely reflects what was already Nigerian and Ethiopian municipal law and national policy. There has not been, as yet, a case of nationalization of foreign private investment in Ethiopia. And when airlines, shipping, and external communications were nationalized by Nigeria, evaluation of assets was made by third parties, the compensation figure was reached between the parties in each case, and the price was paid in convertible funds.

There is further encouragement to American investors in the fact that both Nigeria and Ethiopia are parties to the arrangements recently made under the auspices of the World Bank for the arbitration of disputes between private foreign investors and host countries by a panel chosen from a list of international arbitrators selected by the World Bank.

In exceptional cases, the United States Agency for International Investment has expressed its readiness to guarantee a minimum return on certain investments of social significance. I am referring to a project concerned with building low-cost housing in Addis Ababa.

Finally, a project has been put forward for international insurance against all risks—even a guarantee of a minimum return on investments in developing countries by an international agency acting for a group of developed countries in the West. As yet, however, this is only international law in the making.[3]

More serious than nationalization and socialist tendencies is the danger of hastily accelerated Nigerianization, Ethiopianization, or Africanization generally. Here political pressures are more difficult to resist or contain. The desire to see Nigerians or Ethiopians at the head of industrial enterprise is natural and understandable. What is not sufficiently realized by politicians is that it takes considerable time to achieve entrepreneurial capacity and technical efficiency. However, reason, common sense, and hard experience should demonstrate to foreign investors and to local authorities that it is in their mutual interest to accelerate the training of African nationals within the limits of what is possible and reasonable.

The third handicap is *fear of instability* in developing countries which have barely emerged from a colonial to an independent international status. In some African countries which are still struggling with their growing pains, this fear is real and legitimate. However, no two countries in Africa are alike. Consequently, it is a mistake to try to apply generalizations based on disappointing experiences in certain areas of Africa to countries where conditions are entirely different.

It is my considered opinion that inhibitive cautiousness is not justified in the case of Nigeria and Ethiopia. Risks there certainly are. But there are exceptional opportunities too, which more than counterbalance the risks. Here is what Professor Proehl has to say about Nigeria: "For the prospective investor who reaches an affirmative judgment [and it is believed he can reasonably do so], Nigeria offers substantial inducements."[4]

Still, political uncertainties do exist. In a vast country like Nigeria, in which peoples of different tribes are united in a federation, it is natural that there should be tensions, differences of views and outlook. As in the case of the United States a hundred years ago, the important question was to save the Union. For some time there was talk of secession between the South and the North of Nigeria, but the crisis was overcome and the Union was maintained. Happily, thus far, true statesmanship has prevailed, and it is very much to be hoped that this will continue to be the case. There is a realization among the four regions that the federal political structure of the country is a valuable asset to all Nigerians.

[3]An excellent article on the subject of guarantee of foreign investments appeared recently in the *American Journal of International Law*. Written by William Conant Brewer, Jr. under the title "The Proposal for Investment Guarantees by an International Agency," it may be found in Vol. 58 (January 1964), p. 62.
[4]*Op. cit.*

Except for a short period of Italian occupation before the second World War, Ethiopia has had an independent government for thousands of years. Now the country enjoys the wise rule of an Emperor leading his country into a new era through a process of evolution which reconciles stability and gradual change. There is every reason to believe that this process and Ethiopia's hospitable attitude toward foreign investment will continue.

Thus an objective and balanced appraisal of legal institutions and economic conditions in Nigeria and Ethiopia leads to the conclusion that the opportunities and incentives of investment very much outweigh the handicaps and risks involved.

SOUTH AFRICA: THE COUNTRY AND ITS DEVELOPMENT •

RICHARD MANVILLE

FROM MORE THAN ONE point of view, Africa can be divided into three
parts: a northern Arab-dominated part; a central Negro- (or African-)
dominated part; and a southern European-dominated part. This "third
Africa" comprises the subcontinent more or less marked off geographical-
ly by the South Equatorial Divide, which follows in part the watershed of
the Congo and Zambezi rivers. In a politico-economic sense it is constituted of Portuguese Angola and Mozambique; Zambia; Malawi; Rhodesia; the British territories of Bechuanaland, Basutoland, and Swaziland;
South-West Africa; and the Republic of South Africa.

The Republic of South Africa not only occupies the dominant position
on the subcontinent but also is the most industrially developed country in
the whole of Africa. In fact, economically it is one of the 15 most important countries in the world. Its importance in the African context is
well illustrated in that South Africa, with only 6 percent of the total population and 4 percent of the total area, generates some 20 percent of the
continent's total geographic income and accounts for about 50 percent of
total foreign investment in Africa.

The combination of European entrepreneurial drive, rich natural resources, availability of manpower, temperate physical conditions, political
stability, and unequivocal committal to free private enterprise made this
development possible.

RICHARD MANVILLE is President, Richard Manville Research Inc., International
Marketing Consultants, New York, New York.

NATURAL RESOURCES

To consider first the natural resources, water is South Africa's weakest link, and development will probably be finally determined by the efficiency with which this element is used. With 30 inches of rainfall, given the country's evaporation rate (considered the lower limit of "ample moisture"), only about 11 percent of the Republic can be said to be generously endowed in this respect. As most of this 11 percent consists of mountainous country, the actual available area for farming is very small indeed. More startling is the fact that only 25 percent of the country gets more than 25 inches and nearly 30 percent less than ten inches. It boils down to this: nearly 60 percent of the country is, by all known standards, barren, and nearly 90 percent of the country needs water additional to rainfall for full production or any agriculture at all. A further analysis of climatic conditions is given in Table 1.

It is estimated that only half of the "runoff"—all streams—may be usefully employed; what South Africa has available for conservation from rivers and streams is probably only 3.5 percent of the annual precipitation. The importance of underground water to the Republic is demonstrated by the fact that no less than 70 percent of its surface, which carries more than half of its small stock and almost 50 percent of its cattle, is dependent on underground water for its human and animal populations.

The forest area of the subcontinent stretches in a broken strip from Cape Town to Port Elizabeth, continues in the mountains inland from East London, and then broadens out into an irregular belt along the foothills of the Drakensberg mountain range to the Northern Transvaal. The total area of productive plantation is 2.2 million acres. As a result of optimum conditions, the most productive species of pine trees will yield not less than 250 cubic feet of salable timber, on the average, per acre annually over 25 years. The economic advantage is obvious when compared with the mean incremental rates of all the natural forests in Germany (50 cubic feet), Sweden (37 cubic feet), and the United States (13 cubic feet) per acre annually.

The main South African fishing grounds are the Southwestern Cape coast and the coast of South-West Africa, between the Cape and Walvis Bay, and the extraordinarily rich Agulhas Bank along the Southern Cape coast. The shoals occur mainly between three and ten miles out; the total area amounts to about 1,100 square miles. Conservation measures were introduced in 1953, with the collapse of the California sardine industry fresh in mind, but have been slightly relaxed in recent years, as no marked depletion has become apparent.

COUNTRYWIDE CLIMATIC CONDITIONS

Average annual rainfall for whole country:	17.5 inches
Average daily number of hours of sunshine:	7.5 to 9.4
Average temperatures:	Summer, 72°; winter, 58°
Humidity range:	Interior, 52-60%; coast, 75-85%
Elevation:	Average over 4,000 feet; peaks of 6,000 feet; coastal area 500-600 feet above sea level

TABLE 1

The fishing grounds lie along 2,000 miles of coastline which offers few safe anchorages or natural harbors. There is great need for better fishing harbors, and plans are under way for improvements, including a $9.4-million harbor at Cape Town.

Agriculture has always exercised a dominant influence on the history and economic life of South Africa. Indeed, farming has been a traditional occupation in the country for three centuries, dating back to meager beginnings at the foot of Table Mountain where settlement started. At present it still provides a livelihood for about half the population, but it was only from the latter half of the nineteenth century—after the discovery of diamonds and gold—that agriculture acquired what may be termed commercial status.

After the first stimulus, progress was practically nullified as a result of the Anglo-Boer War (1899-1902), during which agricultural assets were destroyed on a large scale, especially in the northern provinces. World War I brought a new impetus, and in the short space of less than four decades production outstripped the demand of the local market and South Africa established itself as a food-exporting country of no mean importance.

South Africa occupies 473,000 square miles. About 86 percent of the area has summer rainfall and dry winters; of the remainder a small area of 16,000 square miles has year-round rainfall (the extreme south), while 50,000 square miles in the Southwestern Cape have winter rainfall and dry summers. The rainfall declines from east to west as the country flattens, and over a large part of the inland plateau the climate varies from arid to semiarid. Only about 10 percent is under the plough today, and it is estimated that the area cultivated will probably never exceed 15 percent. It follows that a great part of the country is suited only to extensive pastoral farming.

The principal cropping or mixed farming regions are the summer-rainfall plateau of the Transvaal and Orange Free State, the highveld and midlands of Natal, and the winter-rainfall regions of the Southwestern Cape. The last-mentioned, with its Mediterranean climate, is the principal region for the production of winter cereals, deciduous fruits, and wine. Between these main regions to the north and south lies the vast expanse of the arid to semiarid Karoo, which is devoted largely to extensive Merino sheep farming for the production of wool. The far northern and northwestern areas of the Transvaal and Cape are essentially extensive cattle farming regions, while the low country of the Eastern Transvaal is important for the production of citrus fruit, subtropical fruits, and vegetables. The frost-free coastal belt of Natal and the Eastern Cape is well suited to a variety of subtropical fruits and particularly for the production of sugar, citrus, bananas, and pineapples. Despite the limitations of soil conditions, climate, and topography, South African farming can boast a remarkable variety, covering virtually every type of animal, crop, fruit, and vegetable production.

South Africa is a treasure house of base minerals, the most important being uranium, iron ore, chromite, manganese ore, asbestos, copper limestone, phosphates, iron pyrites, and ferroalloys. Some production figures are given in Table 2. About 43 percent of Africa's mineral output is accounted for by the Republic, according to a UN Economic and Social Affairs Department report. The Republic is also one of the few countries in the world which possess within their boundaries all the minerals needed for the alloying of steel.

South Africa is known to possess vast resources of iron ore. In the Cape there are 1.3 billion tons of high-grade ore; there are six billion tons of low-grade ore, 2,000 billion tons of ore with 24 to 40 percent iron con-

MINERAL PRODUCTION

Mineral	Time Period	Amount	Export Value
Pig iron	Year 1965	3,600,000 tons	
Steel	Year 1965	3,450,000 tons	
Ferroalloys	Year 1965	365,000 tons	
Iron ore	Jan.-Sept. 1965	4,767,083 short tons	
Manganese	9 months	1,244,331 short tons	$ 12,196,000
Chrome	9 months	804,806 short tons	$ 5,277,800
Asbestos	9 months	178,406 short tons	$ 23,898,000
Total industrial minerals	9 months		$1,057,266,000

TABLE 2

tent, and 2,200 billion tons of titaniferous ores in the Bushveld Igneous Complex. All resources add up to more than two trillion tons of iron ore!

Manganese is mined extensively. The Postmasburg deposits rank among the finest in the world; among the superior qualities of this manganese is its hardness, which reduces losses in transport to a minimum. Total world annual production of this essential raw material, mainly for consumption in steel plants, amounts to some 14 million tons, of which South Africa supplies one million.

The Republic is in the fortunate position of being able to supply the world with the three principal varieties of asbestos—crocidolite, or blue asbestos; chrysotile; and amosite. The latter variety is mined in the Eastern Transvaal, which is almost the only source in the world for this variety. Chrome ore was first mined in the early twenties, when a few hundred tons were sent to a steelworks at Vereeniging. It is now known that the Transvaal possesses vast resources of chrome ore. Among the base minerals now exported are antimony, clay, corundum, felspar, iron pyrites, mica, titanium, vermiculite, and chrome ore.

INDUSTRIAL ACHIEVEMENT AND POTENTIAL

There are two major projects which will stimulate the development of South Africa. One is the Orange River Project, which was announced in 1962. The 30-year project will cost about $630 million, and the end result will be larger than the Hoover Dam in the United States. The water harnessed through dams, weirs, and tunnels will transform a semidesert into an area of intense agricultural and industrial activity. The first phases have already been started. Eventually, 20 hydroelectric power stations will supply an electricity network extending from the Atlantic to the Indian Ocean. The other large project that has been started is the Pongola Dam on the Transvaal-Natal border, with similar objectives of irrigation, electricity, and industrial expansion.

The forest industry, including its ancillary wood industries, has an annual wage bill of approximately $28 million and gives employment to 110,000 production workers. The afforested area contributes more than $100 million to the country's industrial output.

The total fish catch increased from only 64,000 short tons in 1938 to more than 1.2 million tons in 1963. In 13 years South Africa had increased her annual catch by 600 percent, and in ten years fish exports had risen by 900 percent. South African rock lobster is, of course, a well-known delicacy in the United States.

South Africa's first industrial community emerged with the discovery of

GOLD AND DIAMOND PRODUCTION

[January-September 1965]

	Amount	Value
Diamonds	3,713,602 metric carats	$ 42,595,000
Gold	22,802,489 fine ounces	$801,670,000

TABLE 3

diamonds more than 90 years ago. The country's national income underwent a further change with the discovery of gold in 1886. With this came the introduction of a stable money and credit economy. Within four years, 505 industrial undertakings—dominated by wagon builders and bakers—were setting up factories; transportation and roads grew apace. South Africa and South-West Africa produce a high percentage of gem stones, which makes the diamond output value the highest in the world, although more industrial diamonds are mined in other African territories. (See Table 3 for production figures for gold and diamonds.)

In South Africa, kimberlite deposits are mined at Kimberley in the Northern Cape, Jagersfontein in the Orange Free State, and Premier Mine in the Transvaal. Alluvial and marine terrace deposits are mined on the Vaal-Harts and Orange Rivers, in the Western Transvaal, and in the coastal and desert areas of South-West Africa and the Cape. Nothing quite like the auriferous reefs of South Africa is known anywhere else in the world.

The discovery of gold hastened the opening up of South Africa; today the industry is not only its biggest foreign exchange earner but an important factor in its internal economy. It is the largest single consumer of electricity and spends millions a year on stores, supplies, and agricultural products. The goldfields stretch in a 300-mile semicircle through the Southern Transvaal and Northern Orange Free State. Seventy percent of the gold produced comes from the Transvaal; the biggest reserves of ore are in the Free State, which will eventually yield 350 million fine ounces. A vast industrial complex arose around the goldfields of the Southern Transvaal.

South Africa produces 72 percent of the world's gold outside the Soviet Union. With gold South Africa could, without undue difficulty, pay for the capital goods required to expand total national output. Since the war alone, the gold-mining industry has attracted over $518 million in new capital, more than half of it from foreign countries.

Coal measures in South Africa range from Natal through the Transvaal into the Free State and the Cape Province. Thus there is coal under vast areas of South African soil. The winning of coal has developed into a vigorous industry.

Coal has become increasingly important as a raw material in metallurgical and chemical industries which have mushroomed all over the country. The main users are power stations, which generate the world's cheapest electricity from the low priced coals. (Comparative pithead prices per ton: Transvaal, South Africa, $1.69; Britain, $7.45; Australia, $6.13; United States, $6.02.) Industry is the second largest consumer, followed by South African Railways.

The total value realized for coal, from the earliest records, has been exceeded only by diamonds and gold. South Africa produces about 92 percent of all coal mined in Africa and possesses about 80 percent of the continent's reserves. At the present rate of production South Africa's coal reserves should be sufficient for something like 2,000 years; the established reserves have been estimated at 76,000 billion tons.

The Government-controlled Electricity Supply Commission (ESCOM) supplies about 80 percent of the country's power at an average price of .510c (Rand) per unit—as compared with 1.233c in England and 1.053c to 1.972c in Australia. Major power stations are being erected in the Eastern Transvaal and on other coalfield sites. Some $770 million will be spent over ten years on electricity development.

South Africa has no navigable rivers, so that transportation is by rail, highway, and air. The chief means of transportation is the railroad system, comprising about 14,000 route miles of which about 3,500 miles with heavy traffic density are electrified. The Republic is served by a system of excellent highways. There are approximately 115,000 miles of national and provincial roads, of which some 13,400 miles of surface had been bituminized as of 1963. International airlines and ships operate extensive services. There is also a regular internal service operated by South African Airways.

SOCIO-ECONOMIC FACTORS

Settlement of the Cape, in 1652, was a commercial undertaking. The Dutch East India Company wanted a supply station for ships plying the oriental spice route; Cape Town was the "halfway house." The company, through its monopoly system, persuaded the early settlers to live by agriculture alone. Until 1870, secondary industry was virtually unknown.

The first industrial community emerged, as already mentioned, with the discovery of diamonds and gold. The country's national income, based on self-sufficing agriculture (and that largely pastoral), rapidly rose with

NET DOMESTIC PRODUCT: 1964

		Percent
Agriculture and mining (primary)		21.7
Manufacturing (secondary)		27.8
Commerce and services (tertiary)		28.9
Public sector		21.6
	Total	100*

*100% = $8,534,000,000.

TABLE 4

the changes. The State Treasury soon found itself able to pay for imports without difficulty. A local purchasing power was generated. By 1912 manufacturing industry was responsible for 6.7 percent of the national income; it has now risen to more than 27 percent (see Table 4). The gross value of manufacturing production today averages an estimated $6.09 billion per year as compared with $851 million in 1945. Table 5 shows the rise in gross national product. This phenomenal achievement stands up well to international comparison.

The present national per-capita income of $420 is low compared with, say, those of the United Kingdom ($1,246 in 1963) and other advanced Western nations because of the inclusion of nonwhites, which depresses the average. However, it compares favorably in per-capita income with countries like Italy, Japan, and Australia. It is further expected that by the turn of the century the per-capita income will equal the present British figure.

The earnings of the Bantu have been rising at a much faster rate than those of the white population; for the years 1959-60 and 1960-61 their wages rose twice as fast as real wages paid to whites. The total income of whites since the war has increased by approximately 300 percent and that of the nonwhites by more than 500 percent. A feature of the postwar period has been the vast improvement in the nonwhites' wages and living standards. There is a drive in private industry, encouraged by the Government, to increase the wages of Bantu workers with a view to raising their productivity as well as their purchasing power—which today already approaches the $1-billion mark.

In a country where the relations between management and labor are complicated by the multiracial composition of the population, industrial peace has reigned for more than 30 years. Since 1922 there have been only two big strikes, in 1946 and 1947. These strikes (in the mining industry) were caused by dissension on domestic matters affecting trade union man-

REAL RATE OF GROWTH: GNP

	Percent Increase
1961	4
1962	7
1963	7.5
1964	6.5
Four-year average	6.25

TABLE 5

agement and were not directed against the employers. During 1961, for instance, only 329 whites and 4,662 nonwhites took part in strikes.

Industry in all its branches employs more than 1.7 million workers. As a result of the shortage of white labor, many Bantu have been placed in semiskilled and skilled jobs. According to press reports, certain motor assembly plants which had all white personnel ten years ago now have a 70 percent nonwhite labor force. In the main center of the South African footwear industry, the Eastern Cape, the proportion of white employees dropped from 60 percent to 39.6 percent in ten years—with a corresponding rise in nonwhite employment.

If one considers that the Bantu until quite recently were probably at a lower level of development than the Gallic tribes at the time of Julius Caesar's conquests, the Bantu have indeed adapted themselves remarkably well to factory work. But they still have to develop a great deal before they can equal the efficiency of unskilled labor in Europe and America. In many instances, for example, machines have to be set at a slower pace and operations have to be simplified to bring them within the Bantu's capacity. Textile manufacturers with experience both in South Africa and overseas have reported that after three years of training, Bantu labor attains approximately 75 percent of the efficiency to be found in their factories in Europe.

Against the background of the primitive existence to which they were accustomed under the tribal system, the Bantu's present earnings constitute a very real advance. The general wage level is certainly low, but it is of importance that masses of Bantu, who formerly lived on the verge of starvation when drought and locusts menaced their crops, have within an incredibly short time secured for themselves a regular and stable cash income.

One of the features of South Africa's economic scene is the rapid rate of urbanization. From 1951 to 1960 the total population of the 12 largest cities increased by almost 30 percent. Eighty percent of the country's urban population is concentrated in four major industrial areas: 2.75 million in the Southern Transvaal, one million in the Western Cape, 750,000 in the Durban-Pinetown area of Natal, and approximately 450,000 in Port Elizabeth and East London in the Eastern Cape.

The rapid industrialization of South Africa has revolutionized not only the economic structure of the country but also the traditional way of life of great masses of the population. A generation ago the vast majority of Bantu still lived in rural surroundings, living on a subsistence economy, eking out a living by cultivation of their land in the time-honored way or under improved conditions on white farms. But even those who worked for white employers preferred to return to their tribal homes for long "rest periods" when they had saved sufficient money to stop working. Since those days more than a third of the Bantu population has become urbanized. The total urban Bantu population increased from 900,000 at the outbreak of World War II to over 2.3 million in 1951, and in almost every major town of the Republic Bantu now outnumber the white inhabitants.

Employment has reached the stage of a labor bottleneck, with a shortage of skilled labor in many fields. Unemployment is less than 1 percent. Whereas in 1930 the total number of employees in private industry was 168,400 with $53.2 million paid in salaries and so forth, the total employment in 1965 was one million with $1.4 billion paid in salaries. Over the three years from 1963 through 1965 alone employment went up by 36,-000 (to 483,000) for whites and by more than 200,000 (to 1.5 million) for nonwhites in the major sectors of production, excluding agriculture. The total economically active population in 1970 is projected at 7.077 million.

Private consumer spending increased by 13 percent over 1964 and by 3.5 percent in 1965—after certain restrictions were implemented because of an "overheating economy" and dangers of wage inflation. (Independent economists and the minister of finance have stated that these restrictions have been producing the desired effect.) The net inflow of foreign capital in 1965 amounted to $323.4 million, of which some $70 million represented private long-term investment capital. Buildings completed in 18 principal municipalities during 1965 are valued at $206.5 million—up $49.98 million over the previous year, despite building restrictions.

As far as exports and imports are concerned, preliminary figures for 1965 place exports at $1.46 billion. This represents an increase of only .2 percent over 1964 because of a decline in uranium oxide sales, and in agricultural produce sales as the result of a prolonged drought. Imports during 1965 came to $2.44 billion.

Where necessity dictated it, the State has taken entrepreneurial initiative to establish key industries, always subject to conditions such as the following:

- The enterprise must not be in competition with the private sector.
- It must be a key industry.
- It must have a service motive and not primarily a profit one.
- It must have the deliberate purpose of serving as a driving force for related industries and of helping to develop industry as a whole.
- It must provide related industries with essential materials at a relatively low price.

Industries that arose in this way are ISCOR, the South African Iron and Steel Corporation; SASOL, the South African Coal, Oil and Gas Corporation; FOSKOR, the South African Phosphate Development Corporation; and ESCOM, the Electricity Supply Commission. Another one, Klipfontein Organic Products Corporation, has since been sold to a private consortium.

POPULATION COMPONENTS

Most of the white citizens are descended from early Dutch, French, German, and British settlers, although there are smaller admixtures of other European peoples. The Dutch character of the Cape settlement before the British occupation slowly changed into a distinctly South African one—Afrikanerdom. This was at first broadly categorized under "Boer" (farmer), as these Afrikaners were also known at the turn of the century when they fought the British for their independence. In the late 1880's they were also known as "Afrikaners" among some progressive intellectuals of the Cape who strove for the recognition of their language, Afrikaans, the local development of the Dutch language. After final British occupation social and other conditions fostered a distinction between "Englishman" and "Afrikaner," and a factional friction ensued which has only lately died down. Today the white groups in South Africa live harmoniously with mutual respect for differences in cultural traditions. Both English and Afrikaans are official languages. The language breakdown for the white population is as follows:

Both Afrikaans and English—1.4 percent
Afrikaans—58 percent
English—37.3 percent
Other—3.3 percent

About the time the Cape was settled, in the second half of the seventeenth century, successive waves of migrating black peoples entered the northern and eastern areas of present-day South Africa. They were tribes forced down by as yet undetermined factors—spreading desert conditions in the north, internecine wars, or the need for new pastures for their cattle, perhaps. The Bantu, who are mainly encountered in Africa south of the equator, are believed to have originated from an admixture of Hamitic and Negroid peoples. Some South African tribes have click sounds in their languages, suggesting contact with Bushmen or Hottentots in the early stages of their journey southward. The migration followed three main "streams" from the vicinity of the Great Lakes of Central Africa. Briefly, one group settled in Angola, farther south and in the Congo Basin; the second, or Sotho, group finally settled in Bechuanaland, Basutoland, and parts of the Transvaal and Northern Cape Province; the third, or Nguni, group moved down the eastern seaboard into Natal and the Northeastern Cape. Others of this group settled in Swaziland.

In the second half of the eighteenth century sporadic meetings between white groups—hunters and explorers—and black parties grew into a constant contact situation as the masses of white farmers and black tribes were drawn up facing each other across the Fish River, some 600 miles from Cape Town. There was no more free land on which to maneuver, in a manner of speaking, and two totally different cultures came into definite and permanent contact. This area of first permanent contact today is obviously the most "civilized" in Western terms and has therefore been the first Bantu homeland to attain self-government. The Transkei supports the Xhosa peoples, a group of Nguni tribes, who today boast their own Western-style parliament and administration.

The technological overweight of the Western society was naturally dominant in the contact situation, and a variety of benevolent paternalism toward the Bantu developed after peace with the warring tribes was attained. Absorption of unskilled black labor into white agriculture and, later, industry has worked to change the way of life of the Bantu to no mean extent. The Government policy of separate development aims at safeguarding those cultural aspects of traditional Bantu life which are of spiritual value while leading the masses of black people into a modern technological society.

Linguistic and cultural differences between the Bantu nations themselves may be illustrated by using Europe as an example. The Nguni and Sotho groups differ as much from one another as, say, the Germanic and Latin groups in Europe, while subgroups such as the western and southern Sotho differ, perhaps, to the extent that the Dutch and Flemish-speaking peoples of the Low Countries differ from one another. Many Bantu can speak either Afrikaans or English or both, but among themselves they usually speak one of the many Bantu languages. At the mines a lingua franca, called Fanagalo, was developed to enable different Bantu to communicate with one another and with the whites.

Two other nonwhite population groups of importance are found in the Republic: the Cape Coloreds, as South Africans call them, and Asiatics. The Cape Coloreds are mulattoes formed by the admixture of Bantu, Hottentot, and slave blood, with an occasional infusion of white blood. The group also contains a Malay Moslem faction. The Asiatics are mostly Indians brought to the Natal sugar cane fields in the 1870's as indentured laborers by the British administration of the time. Also included are some 5,000 Chinese.

Finally, there are the foreign-born Bantu, illegal entrants attracted by South Africa's favorable labor conditions. It is estimated that this group numbers approximately 830,000.

The estimated population figures are as follows:
Whites—3,250,000 (19.0 percent)
Bantus—11,645,000 (68.2 percent)
Coloreds—1,648,000 (9.7 percent)
Asiatics—522,000 (3.1 percent)

The largest Bantu nations are the Xhosa, of whom there are 3,044,000, and the Zulu, who number 2,867,000. For population density see Table 6.

As might be expected, these peoples represent a variety of religious faiths. The bulk of the Afrikaans-speaking whites belong to the Dutch Reformed Churches, and the English-speaking to the Anglican, Methodist, Presbyterian, and Roman Catholic churches. The bulk of the Christianized Bantu belong to the Dutch Reformed, Anglican, and Methodist churches, and to various Bantu Separatist groups. The Jewish, Moslem,

ESTIMATED POPULATION DENSITY

	Number per Square Mile
Whites	6.88
Coloreds	3.49
Asiatics	1.1
Bantus	24.65
Total	36.12*

*Compared with 855 in the Netherlands and 567 in Britain.

TABLE 6

and oriental faiths are well represented. According to the Population Census of 1960 some 3.5 million people professed "other beliefs" or "no religion," which would include primitive animism and other variations of paganism.

With regard to the political situation in South Africa, on March 30, 1966 the ruling party was returned to power with an extended majority. The National Party, ruling since 1948, holds 126 seats in the Lower House; the main opposition, the United Party, 39; and the Progressive Party, one. There are four white members representing the Colored community, making the "Volksraad" a chamber of 170 seats.

The following is a list of organizations that will provide information about South Africa for the prospective investor or business executive.

Associated Chambers of Commerce, Box 687, Johannesburg, S.A.

South African Federated Chamber of Industries, Box 3531, Johannesburg, S.A.

South Africa Foundation, Box 7006, Johannesburg, S.A.

Richard Manville Research Inc., 230 Park Avenue, New York, New York 10017.

In addition, the addresses of specific industry associations are available from the South African Consulate General, 655 Madison Avenue, New York, New York 10021.

AN ECONOMIC PICTURE OF
SOUTH AFRICA ·

H. P. VAN AGGELEN

AIDED BY foreign technical skill and capital, the African continent is rapidly breaking away from its economic isolation. In a relatively short period vast development has taken place in many parts of this continent with a consequent increase in general living standards and marketing opportunities.

With its proportionately large white population and great mineral wealth, the Republic of South Africa has become the leading and by far the most economically advanced and prosperous country in Africa. Development was particularly strong in the postwar period when the discovery and exploitation of new, rich goldfields and a great industrial expansion profoundly affected the whole economic structure of the country.

Foreign capital has played an important role in the economic development of South Africa. As the free world's major gold producer, the Republic is sometimes referred to as a "gilt-edged" country which offers many profitable investment opportunities. An official census of the foreign liabilities and assets of the Republic of South Africa shows that at the end of 1964 total foreign investments in the country amounted to approximately $4.75 billion.

A breakdown of South Africa's total foreign indebtedness, according to countries, clearly reveals the dominating position of the United Kingdom as a source of capital with a contribution of nearly $3 billion, or about 60 percent of the total. Continental Western Europe and the United States were close seconds in order of importance with investments of about $750 million each, equivalent to approximately 28 percent of South Africa's total foreign liabilities.

H. P. VAN AGGELEN is Representative, Netherlands Bank of South Africa Limited, New York, New York.

Industry. Within a few decades South Africa has become a major industrial nation—in fact, one of the most industrialized countries in the Southern Hemisphere. Private industry's contribution of about 25 percent to total geographical income is higher than that of any other national branch of economic activity.

The extent of South Africa's postwar industrial growth is clearly shown by the considerable rise in the gross value of output of all private industries from $1,245 million in 1946-1947 to over $5,000 million in 1963-1964. This is only partly the result of an increase in the general price level.

The nucleus of South Africa's heavy industry is the integrated iron and steel works of the South African Iron and Steel Industrial Corporation Ltd. (ISCOR), a Government-sponsored and controlled undertaking which started production in 1934 and has since expanded considerably. ISCOR's steel production in 1963-1964 was nearly 2.8 million ingot tons, with sales exceeding $216 million.

The total domestic requirements of rolled and drawn steel products were estimated roughly at 2.6 million tons in 1963-1964. South African producers supplied about 91 percent of this total, to which ISCOR contributed approximately 77 percent compared with 36 percent and 28 percent, respectively, immediately before the Second World War.

Under a modernization scheme completed in 1961 at a cost of nearly $157 million, the capacity of ISCOR's steel output reached 2.4 million ingot tons per annum. A further expansion program at a cost of $785 million is being undertaken which will increase steel ingot production to almost 4.5 million tons by 1973.

Local steel prices are among the lowest in the world. This has greatly encouraged the establishment and development of the metal, machinery, and engineering industries. Since the Second World War, light as well as heavy industries have expanded considerably; nowadays a wide variety of goods is manufactured locally. To mention only a few items, production includes textile piece goods, clothing, footwear, furniture, toys, household articles, paper, chemicals, fertilizers, food, and beverages.

An important motor-car assembly and ancillary industry also developed in the postwar period; and, in view of the Government's policy to encourage the use of South African materials, there is increasing scope for further expansion in the motor-component industry. Several motor-car assemblies are engaged in expansion programs. These involve total capital investments of more than $150 million for the local manufacture of an impressive range of motor components, including engines, gear boxes, rear axles, and body pressings. Some models have already attained a local-materials content of more than 45 percent.

In the chemical field the many by-products available from SASOL's oil-from-coal plant have increased the potential for further development. Examples are the recent establishment of a synthetic rubber plant near SASOL's area of operation at an overall cost of over $40 million and the erection of plants for the production of chemicals such as polyethylene, used in the manufacture of plastics, and cyanide. The establishment, some years ago, of the Government-sponsored Phosphate Development Corporation (Pty) Ltd. (FOSKOR) for the local production of superphosphates has benefited the domestic fertilizer industry. An $8.40 million fertilizer factory for the production of superphosphates is in the course of construction near FOSKOR's plant. Another venture, in which American capital and know-how will be invested, has recently been announced.

In addition, a $104 million copper mine, backed by substantial overseas mining interests, is nearing completion in the area.

In most instances domestic requirements are adequately catered to. Since the Second World War there has also been a significant increase in South Africa's industrial exports. The development of export markets for South Africa's growing industrial output is promoted by the active support of the Government. With its relatively cheap and abundant labor, power, and raw material resources, this country has strong competitive advantages.

Many industries in South Africa are subsidiaries or offshoots of overseas manufacturing concerns which have been impressed by local marketing opportunities and available resources. South Africa's geographical position, far from possible centers of world conflict yet strategically placed between the Western and Eastern Hemispheres, also proved to be a strong inducement to foreign industrialists to decentralize their interests and extend their activities to this country.

Of the four major industrial areas in South Africa the Southern Transvaal, including Johannesburg and Pretoria, is by far the most important. Two-fifths of all private local industrial establishments are situated in this part of the country. The other regions are Cape Town, Durban, and Port Elizabeth. The concentration of industry in a few parts of the country has created certain problems and put a heavy strain on available resources, particularly water. Whenever possible, the decentralization of industry to less developed areas with suitable raw materials and more abundant supplies of water and unskilled labor is encouraged officially.

To foster further industrialization, special investment incentives have been introduced by the Government. These provide for an initial allowance of 15 percent and for an investment allowance of 20 percent on new plant and equipment in addition to the annual rate of depreciation normally applicable. Furthermore, an investment allowance of 10 percent is deductible from the cost of erecting new factory premises, as an added incentive.

These concessions have been further extended with respect to the border areas. These are regions situated near the nonwhite (Bantu) territories, and their development is intended to serve the dual purpose of providing suitable employment for the large unskilled Bantu population in its own homelands and to further the aims of industrial decentralization. Additional incentives for the establishment of industries in these regions include assistance in the provision of water, power, transport, and housing; they also provide for the laying out of planned industrial sites, the erection and letting of factory buildings, and, in special cases, partial reimbursement of building costs.

Trade. In terms of purchasing power the Republic of South Africa is the most important market on the African continent. Total personal income exceeds $8 billion a year, while personal consumption expenditures run well into $6 billion a year.

Under a scheme sponsored by the Industrial Development Corporation (IDC), with the cooperation of the commercial banks, the Credit Guarantee Insurance Corporation of Africa Limited, and the financial authorities, medium-term finance is extended at low cost to local industrialists for the export of capital goods on a credit basis. In selected cases credit facilities, termed "financial credits," are made available direct to the foreign borrower for more than five years where such terms and matching insurance cover are clearly justified and where the project has a substantial foreign exchange earning potential.

Special tax concessions are made to exporters in their drive to develop new export markets.

Finance. The heavy investment activity in the Republic, reflecting the rate of postwar economic expansion, is illustrated by statistics relating to gross domestic capital formation.

As is usual in young countries endowed with vast potentialities, South Africa's own financial resources were far too limited at first to initiate and sustain large-scale expansion, which was only made possible through attraction of overseas investment funds. With the increase in national production, general prosperity, and living standards, domestic savings have, however, gradually risen to substantial proportions.

While complete financial self-sufficiency has not yet been reached and foreign investment capital will still be needed to assist in a continued expansion of the national economy, South Africa is now in a much stronger position than ever before to finance her own development. This has made for greater internal monetary and economic stability by diminishing the influence of unpredictable fluctuations in the supply of overseas capital.

The expansion of secondary industry in South Africa was greatly assisted by the Industrial Development Corporation of South Africa Ltd., established by the Government in 1940. Its function is to finance new and existing industrial ventures which are conducted in accordance with sound business principles and contribute to meeting the country's economic requirements. The corporation's issued capital amounts to more than $200 million, and it has invested about $250 million since its establishment. In 1957 it assisted in promoting the formation of the Industrial Finance Corporation of South Africa Ltd., with a capital of $14 million, in which privately owned financial institutions hold a majority interest. The main function of this organization is to foster industrial expansion by providing venture capital to new or existing industrial enterprises with good profit potential and experienced and able management.

In addition to these and other institutions which aim more specifically to meet the demand for medium- and long-term finance, a number of financial organizations specialize in the provision of short-term credit. Foremost among them are the commercial banks, which are also authorized dealers in foreign exchange, operating branch systems which cover the whole of South Africa and South-West Africa. The four main commercial banks are Barclays Bank D.C.O., Netherlands Bank of South Africa Limited, The Standard Bank of South Africa Limited, and Volkskas Limited. Central banking operations are conducted by the South African Reserve Bank, which is the Government's banker and performs all the functions normally associated with central banking.

Particularly in recent years, a more active money market has developed in South Africa, with full acceptance and discount facilities provided. The commercial banks have also extended their services to include, either directly or indirectly through subsidiaries, installment credit financing, leasing, factoring, merchant banking, and especially medium and longer-term financing.

Taxation. The level of taxation in South Africa compares favorably with that in most other countries. Basically, individuals as well as companies pay tax in the Republic on income which is derived, or deemed to be derived, from a source within the country, no matter where the recipient of this income resides. But, with certain exceptions, dividend income received by individuals from abroad also is subject to tax.

With the exception of those engaged in gold mining, all companies pay tax at a flat rate, whereas a progressive rate applies to individuals. Most companies pay 30 percent. Diamond-mining companies, however, pay 45 percent, and for gold-mining companies the rate is calculated by a special formula.

Currency. On February 14, 1961, South Africa decimalized her monetary system. The Rand, divided into 100 cents, became the new monetary unit on a conversion basis of two Rand equaling one South African pound. R1 is equivalent to approximately U.S. $1.40.

Exchange control. All foreign exchange transactions in South Africa, whether of a current or capital nature and irrespective of currency area, are subject to treasury control. All buying and selling of foreign currency has to be effected through the intermediary of authorized dealers in foreign exchange; all commercial and merchant banks in South Africa have been appointed authorized dealers in foreign exchange.

The export of all capital funds, whether resident- or nonresident-owned, is subject to strict control and official approval, but the South African Government has never departed from its traditional policy of allowing the unhampered repatriation to its point of origin of the current earnings on any capital investments made in this country by nonresidents. The exchange control authorities will, under current regulations and on application through an authorized dealer in exchange, also not object to the repatriation of foreign loans on due date provided in general that repayment is made from available cash funds and requires no recourse to local borrowing.

Payments, by South African residents, having to do with royalities, designs, patents, trademarks, and the like also are subject to specific approval by the exchange control authorities. In general, sympathetic consideration is given to applications in those cases where the acquisition of such rights would be in the interest of local industries.

Other controls. Private enterprise is the dominant form of economic organization in South Africa. The creation of conditions conducive to expansion over as wide a front as possible has been one of the main objectives of Government economic policy.

No specific restrictions are placed on the establishment or the expansion of commercial or industrial undertakings, except that official approval must be obtained first if any foreign exchange expenditure is involved. Free private enterprise is the cornerstone of the country's truly fantastic development over the past decades. The investment climate is a good one, as is shown by officially published figures indicating that profits on invested capital average 27 percent, while dividend returns average well over 12 percent. The Republic of South Africa has a highly developed and stable economy and a well-established commercial and financial framework, in addition to a fast-growing industrial apparatus which complements and is beginning to overshadow the very important mining and agricultural sectors.

DOING BUSINESS IN AFRICA •

LUDWIG E. ARMERDING

OF THE POLITICAL, social, and economic upheavals that have characterized the years following World War II, none have been quite so momentous as those experienced by the continent of Africa. With no fewer than 34 former colonial possessions gaining sovereign status in slightly over a decade, Africa has been the scene of history's most massive transfer of political responsibility. Economically, progress has not been quite so dramatic, yet the continent's industrial and commercial potential has proved increasingly attractive to overseas companies. Pfizer's growth in Africa reflects this changing climate. The company now has manufacturing plants in four African countries and marketing organizations throughout the continent—employing more than 800 people. Africa received separate status as a Pfizer area in 1963, with headquarters in Nairobi. While total sales are still small in comparison to the volume of company business in industrially developed parts of the world, all indications point to an excellent rate of growth.

GROWTH OF PFIZER'S AFRICAN OPERATIONS

Before 1951 Pfizer's overseas activities were limited to relatively modest exports of products in demand with little or no effort to stimulate such demand. In 1951 the Pfizer International organization was established to undertake a *positive* role in international business and to develop the sales of the company's products in all countries outside the United States. The first effort in Africa was in the Union of South Africa, where a distributor was appointed. After a few years, he was superseded by Pfizer International's own company. The second step came after Pfizer International

---

LUDWIG E. ARMERDING is Area Manager, Africa, Pfizer International, Nairobi, Kenya.

entered France in 1952 with production and marketing. Under an agreement with partners, responsibility was assigned for the development of the then French countries in Africa to the French business. Little was done in the rest of the continent until 1956, when responsibility for its development was placed with Pfizer International's European area organization. Apart from the then French countries, which were supplied out of France, the needs of the continent were met from British sources or from a distribution center which had been set up in Belgium depending on currency availabilities.

Following the assignment of responsibility to area management in Europe in 1956, a complete review of the prospects on the continent was made. The most important result of this review was the realization of the long-range potential of the African countries south of the Sahara and north of the Zambezi, and the determination to start developing seriously the Pfizer business in them.

First, distributorship agreements were made with established European trading companies in key locations. Under these agreements, the distributor received the Pfizer agency on a nonexclusive basis, leaving the company the right to sell to government or independent organizations. The distributor guaranteed to carry three months' stock and replacement according to Pfizer supply schedules. Pfizer, for its part, supplied the distributor with promotion and detailing material and sent its own medical or technical advisers to instruct representatives of the distributor's organization. Mailings to doctors, pharmacists, and hospitals were made directly from Pfizer organizations in Europe. Distributors received a 10 percent commission on sales.

This system was all right as a start, but its limitations soon became obvious. As Africa's "wind of change" hastened political, economic, and social progress on the continent, it became increasingly clear that if the company were to keep pace with these developments as they affected local markets, the distributorship machinery would have to be supplanted by the application of Pfizer's basic overseas business policy: establishing wholly owned subsidiaries in as many countries as possible.

Another factor influenced this review of policy. Although doing business through distributors was safe and even profitable, the system contained a serious built-in shortcoming that threatened to retard growth. Normally, the distributor organizations represented up to 20 or 30 overseas companies. Owing to growing demand for Pfizer products, the company's product range broadened, but no guarantee was given by the distributor that all of these lines would receive equal promotional attention. Indeed, the tendency was to favor those products yielding the highest profit margin to the distributor.

Accordingly, it was decided that Pfizer organizations should be established in major African markets as soon as feasible, and that contracts with local distributors should be terminated as each individual subsidiary came into being. Initially, seven companies were formed in Africa outside the Francophone area. In the latter region, arrangements with Pfizer's French organization remained in effect because of the interrelation of former French colonies with the metropolitan country—particularly in regard to licensing and import regulations.

The first objectives of the new subsidiaries were of a foundation-laying nature. Three goals received particular attention: (1) establishing companies within the markets to satisfy local governments' plans for economic development, (2) learning the most suitable methods of marketing and merchandising to the indigenous populations, and (3) training nationals of these countries for the eventual assumption of all managerial responsibilities. These aims were considered important if a Pfizer organization was to set down roots in any country in accordance with the company's corporate citizenship philosophy. Therefore, while a reasonable turnover and a reasonable profit were sought, management was prepared to forgo immediate profits, provided tangible progress toward the above three objectives became evident in a reasonable period of time.

How did these subsidiaries succeed in putting themselves on their feet? How did they meet the diverse and often unique problems of administration and marketing confronted in Africa? How were their operations adapted to conform with increasingly rapid economic and political change?

From the standpoint of administration and marketing, Pfizer's Ghana subsidiary may be considered quite representative. Although there has been no vertical development leading to local manufacture in this relatively small organization, its growth points up many of the difficulties—and rewards—encountered by U.S. firms entering the African market.

GHANA: THE COUNTRY AND THE MARKET

The Republic of Ghana, situated on the west coast of Africa, covers an area of 91,000 square miles. It is bordered by the Atlantic Ocean on the south and by the Ivory Coast, Voltaic Republic, and Togo on the west, north, and east respectively. It is a sub-Sahara country, its vegetation ranging from tropical rain forest in the south to semidesert in the north. Temperatures vary between 77°F. and 105°F. according to season.

Humidity in the southern regions often averages 80 to 95 percent. The population is approximately eight million and consists of five principal tribal groups. There are three main local tongues, and the official language, English, is spoken by more than 50 percent of the people.

Formerly the British Gold Coast Colony, Ghana in 1957 became the first European possession in tropical Africa to receive independence. In 1960 it became a republic within the British Commonwealth.

The capital and main trading center is Accra, with a population of approximately 350,000, followed by the cities of Kumasi and Takoradi, with populations of 220,000 and 120,000 respectively. There are two ports, Tema in the east and Takoradi in the west. Railways link Accra, Tema, Takoradi, and Kumasi. Tarmac roads exist between all the principal cities and larger towns.

Basically an agricultural nation at present, Ghana grows 30 percent of the world's cocoa, which comprises her chief export; other natural resources include timber, diamonds, gold, and manganese. However, the key to Ghana's economic future is found in huge bauxite deposits which will transform the country into a major aluminum producer, thus removing the risky reliance on cocoa—with its fluctuating world price—as the principal source of revenue. The $300 million Volta River hydroelectric project is to provide low-cost energy for an aluminum plant now under construction at Tema. It will also increase the national power supply by about 500 percent and stimulate the growth of other local industries. Several by-products of the Volta project are certain to further diversify and strengthen the economy. Lake Volta, the world's largest man-made lake, will create an important fishing industry, while a vast irrigation scheme will permit large-scale cotton and sugar cane production. The same irrigation project is also expected to yield substantial quantities of staples for local consumption, thereby reducing food import expenditures. The port of Tema, it should be added, is an artificial harbor that was constructed to handle aluminum exports, but it has also become Ghana's chief entrepot for all overseas trade, removing much of the burden from the overcrowded and inadequate docking and cargo-handling facilities at Takoradi.

Ghana's per capita annual income in 1960 was $185, twice that of nearly all other African states south of the Sahara (except South Africa). General education is at a high level; according to Government sources, 85 percent of Ghanaian children under 14 years of age are in school. The people are flexible and good-natured, many of them with high levels of professional skill.

Long-standing commercial links with the West have made Ghana one of Africa's most promising markets; American and European products can be introduced here with less difficulty than in most other regions of Africa. Ghana's main trading partners for the past 15 years have been the United Kingdom, the United States (which imports 35 percent of the country's cocoa production), West Germany, and Japan. Among the U.S. companies established in Ghana are Esso, Kaiser, and Union Carbide.

This, however, is one side of the coin. Ghana's market situation since 1957 has taken on a number of unsettling characteristics, influenced largely by political developments. On the eve of independence, Britain left Ghana with an exchange balance of $518 million, a smoothly functioning government apparatus managed by British nationals in key administrative positions, and a well-trained Ghanaian civil service. Shortly thereafter, however, the Africanization program was accelerated, replacing expatriates with Ghanaians, some of whom were insufficiently prepared for many top-level posts. The introduction of a one-party system placed all power in the hands of President Nkrumah, who did not hesitate to impose police-state methods (notably preventive detention laws) on the entire country. Large amounts of Government funds went into "prestige" investments, of which Ghana Airways is typical. A growing number of barter agreements with Eastern European countries reflected the Government's (which is to say Nkrumah's) political leanings. Russian and Chinese advisers appeared on the scene, and their counsel generally conflicted with that of the Western advisers still in the country.

All this helped create a confused business situation, characterized by conflicting Government policies that veered from permissiveness to rigid economic control. Import licenses were introduced. Exchange control approval was necessary to transfer payment for imports. Shortages of products increased and began to show their effects on the country's economic machinery. The Government continued to overspend on "status" projects, raised taxes, stopped transfers of profits for expatriate companies, increased the number of barter contracts, and used prefinancing institutes in France and Switzerland for financing imports against future cocoa crops. Reserves plummeted to the vanishing point.

To say that these developments brought on a marked loss of Western confidence in Ghana's economic stability is to make a gross understatement. However, disenchantment with Nkrumah's "Animal Farm" was also shared by most Ghanaians, and his removal in the recent army coup may very well prove to be the first step toward the revival of a healthy business climate.

PFIZER IN GHANA

Despite Nkrumah's antagonism toward the West, improved health services have always been a priority target of the Ghana Government, and Pfizer could ill afford to overlook this market. In 1963, Ghana had 520 practicing doctors (Ghanaian and expatriate), 350 pharmacists (all Ghanaian), and more than 1,500 qualified nurses. Hospitals, varying in the quality of their facilities and service, are established in the main centers, and smaller hospitals and health stations—operated by the Government, missions, and private organizations—have done much to improve health in outlying regions. The Government is the main purchaser of pharmaceutical and medicinal preparations—40 to 55 percent of the total—while importers handle the remainder for distribution to retail outlets. No local manufacture of health products existed until 1965.

In 1958 Pfizer established a company in Ghana as a wholly owned subsidiary. Capital paid in was $14,000, with credit given to import goods from Belgian and U.K. subsidiaries. The manager, a former British colonial civil servant, had spent more than 15 years in West Africa. Although his business experience was not extensive (he had been an education officer), it was felt that his extensive familiarity with local affairs would be an overriding asset at a time when such knowledge was vital to the launching of a new company. Moreover, close guidance was to be provided from Pfizer regional headquarters in Europe.

Office and storage facilities were rented in Accra, and five employees were engaged. Staff included a storekeeper with a pharmacist's certificate, this being required by the Government for individuals in charge of drug product storage and sales; an accountant-bookkeeper; a female secretary; a pharmaceutical sales representative qualified as a pharmacist; and an agricultural-veterinary sales representative. All, with the exception of the secretary, were Ghanaians.

Business volume, when Pfizer terminated its contract with the distributor, did not cover the expenses of the newly formed company, and a loss occurred in the first year of the subsidiary's operations. One product accounted for 85 percent of sales; 70 percent of total turnover came from purchases by Government agencies.

Government business was the responsibility of the manager, who also visited mission hospitals and pharmacists with his pharmaceutical sales representative. Later an expatriate physician served as a consultant, training pharmaceutical sales personnel for their field work, and after the first year another pharmaceutical sales representative was appointed. Although three men, including the manager, were promoting drug products in the company's second year of operations, results did not show a significant improvement over the first year.

In 1960, the regional director came to the conclusion that sales development in the Ghana subsidiary required a manager with more practical business experience. Owing to the absence of a qualified expatriate, responsibility for the Ghana organization was placed in the hands of the Pfizer manager for Northeast Africa, who arranged to visit Accra personally every other month. At the same time, a British expatriate was transferred from the Pfizer organization in Angola and made supervisor of local operations under the direction of the Northeast Africa manager. Concurrently, staff was increased by two: a pharmaceutical sales representative and a bookkeeper. Under this new arrangement, sales increased by 60 percent although no profit was realized.

In 1962 the Northeast African manager was relieved of his Ghana assignment so that he could concentrate exclusively on his own region. The expatriate supervisor was at the same time transferred to Lagos, Nigeria, to take over the company's office there. However, he also remained in charge of the Ghana market, visiting Accra one week out of every month; in his absence, managerial responsibilities were in the hands of a Ghanaian pharmaceutical sales representative who had been appointed sales supervisor.

The Ghana organization once more became autonomous in 1963, and a new manager was appointed. With the aim of making progress toward the appointment of a Ghanaian general manager, the Ghanaian sales manager was sent to Europe for a year's further training, since he seemed specially fitted for the general managership. (He later decided to stay in Europe longer and pursue a university course.) Concurrently, to meet the demands of anticipated growth, total employment was brought up to 21. Staff now included five sales representatives (three pharmaceutical and two agricultural) and one medical adviser, the work of the latter being divided between the Ghana and Nigeria organizations. The only expatriate was the newly appointed general manager.

During 1963-1964—the first year following this reorganization—the volume of Government business declined, but sales to the private market increased sufficiently to enable total volume to rise by 150 percent, leaving the company with a reasonable profit after all deductions. For the first time these earnings reflected the real potential of the Ghana market. A wider range of products was introduced, and approximately 30 percent of all sales came from the new lines. While the introduction of import licenses and exchange control by the Government held earnings down, the company's breakthrough appeared to justify plans for considering the establishment of a local plant to produce pharmaceutical, veterinary, agricultural, and consumer products from bulk material.

The manager appointed in 1963 was willing to stay for only two years and moved to Nairobi area headquarters in 1965. He was replaced by another expatriate (with a banking background which would be useful if inflation continued at the then current rate). The local staff has continued to make excellent progress in developing management skills in all aspects of the business, and it is felt that 100 percent Ghanaian management can well be expected in the reasonably near future.

PROBLEMS OF THE GHANA OPERATION

The market. The company's pharmaceutical product market in Ghana is composed chiefly of doctors, in both private practice and Government service; pharmacists; mission hospitals; and various Government purchasing offices. Agricultural and veterinary products are sold mainly to Government agencies, farm cooperative societies, the country's 12 veterinarians, and a large number of individual farmers.

Certain problems of distribution arise from physical environment. Communications cannot always be relied on: heavy rains will sometimes put telephones out of order for several days; mail and telegrams are easily lost. Accordingly, it is practice to send confirmatory copies of all correspondence. Because of overtaxed port facilities, imports of goods often meet with delays, confronting the company with the problem of empty shelves; inventories have therefore been increased from three to six months. We must also take into account the fact that storage conditions are often unsuited to products with expiry dates—for example, antibiotics. Thus all stocks are usually sent to the field earlier than would normally be the case. But despite these not inconsiderable difficulties, distribution of products can be described as fair.

All of Pfizer's Ghanaian advertising is produced in Accra, and problems are encountered here also. Paper shortages often delay printing. Four-color reproduction facilities are nonexistent. Proofs have to be returned up to ten times before they are entirely correct. Yet the company feels that the policy of encouraging local business will, over the long haul, enhance our position in Ghana.

One of our more vexing dilemmas concerns patents. Although our patents are registered in Ghana, local authorities tend to ignore the company's rights and buy products from other sources, such as Italy and Eastern Europe, partly, perhaps, because of examples set by the British Government with regard to Pfizer patents in the United Kingdom but also because of nonacceptance of the philosophy underlying the patent system.

Collection of payments from the farming community and cooperatives is as a rule more difficult than from European trading houses. This is due partly to a frequent lack of immediately available funds but also to a different approach to doing business: many of Africa's buying and selling traditions are geared to a relatively unsophisticated barter philosophy that has not yet vanished entirely from the commercial scene. Payment from Government agencies can normally be expected in approximately three to six months.

Like any established pharmaceutical firm with operations in Africa—or anywhere, for that matter!—Pfizer often encounters competition from inferior products. Wholesalers and retailers frequently accept the prices recommended for our various ethical and O.T.C. lines, but simultaneously offer under-the-counter substitutes from less reliable sources at lower prices—with the dealer nonetheless realizing a much greater profit. It is fairly common among dealers in Ghana and elsewhere in Africa to buy goods on credit at 100, sell at 95 or 98 against cash, and buy other goods for cash at 100 but sell against cash at 150.

Expatriate personnel. If the managerial shifts described earlier suggest a game of corporate musical chairs, this is not due entirely to the normal difficulties surrounding the establishment of any new overseas company. Certain aspects of Africa itself militate against finding qualified expatriate managers who are willing to accept extended assignments on that continent. Climatic conditions, as a rule, are anything but conducive to long-term residence by expatriates. Education presents even more serious problems: despite Africa's by now celebrated thirst for educational progress, schools, by Western standards, are often inadequate above primary level. The traditional practice among expatriates is to educate their children in local primary schools and then send them to high school at home. This tends to curtail sharply a manager's term of African service. Married managers must also consider their wives' comfort and convenience. While there is plenty of help available for the housewife, facilities for shopping, as well as the quality and availability of grocery and other home products, generally leave much to be desired, at least in the eyes of housewives newly arrived from a world of supermarkets.

Most important of all, however, the expatriate manager is often concerned whether the acceptance of such inconveniences will assist or retard his advancement within the organization. He may feel that he is isolated from the mainstream of company growth and apprehensive lest he lose touch with business developments in his home country with the consequence that he may be passed over when vacancies appear in positions of greater responsibility elsewhere.

These are matters of legitimate concern to any multinational organization, and Pfizer has taken a number of steps to alleviate them. Managers in Africa are allowed a month's leave every six months; to help overcome the fear that an African assignment is by definition a career *cul de sac,* one week of each leave is spent in a Pfizer area headquarters, usually New York or Nairobi, thus enabling the manager to keep abreast of developments throughout the organization. Further, with the twin goal of utilizing the manager's abilities to the fullest and providing equal opportunity for advancement at all executive levels, a program is being developed whereby these individuals will be sent to top management courses at various organization headquarters. Finally, with the large number of relatively small but nevertheless complex operations in Africa, Pfizer is able to offer management positions with real responsibility at a relatively young age. This possibility has attracted a number of young men with good university records as a good start to their careers.

Africanization. It has already been noted that a major aspect of the Ghana organization's development was to train Ghanaian employees for posts at all managerial levels, with the ultimate objective of placing total responsibility for the company's operation in Ghanaian hands. Pfizer's corporate citizenship policy applies no less in Africa than anywhere else, although target dates for these goals are not established, for the obvious reason that the nationals of some countries, by virtue of insufficient background in modern business methods, may require more time before they can assume these responsibilities.

In no part of the world does the success of training local personnel depend so much on the abilities of expatriates as in Africa. Besides the usual qualities of experience and leadership, American and European managers in Africa must above all possess a sense of balance in human relations. It can be calamitous for the growth of their organizations if their attitudes are shaped by certain paternalistic notions that gained currency—and were sometimes even encouraged—in colonial times: "They're decent chaps but lazy." "They don't really care about money; they'll quit in the middle of a job if they've earned the price of a bottle of beer." "No initiative. They can imitate what you're doing quite well, but that's as far as it goes." To be guided by such Kiplingesque notions is not merely a human affront; from a very practical business standpoint, it is to court serious trouble from governments justifiably sensitive to their citizens' recent status as "natives" in the eyes of whites.

At the same time, a manager will not serve his company's best interests by adopting an idealistic attitude that turns its back on certain undeniable shortcomings among many African employees, whether executive, technical, or clerical. To a point, the above derogatory comments have a basis in fact, not because of any underlying racial inferiority but simply because during colonial rule Africans were given virtually no incentive or opportunity to move from an age-old tribal culture to the industrialized ways of the West. Now that such opportunities are found in ever-growing abundance, new problems arise—notably a tendency on the part of some Western-trained employees to make unreasonable salary and promotion demands—while many of the earlier ineptitudes remain. But it must be remembered that these are the inevitable concomitants of adjustment. An African is no less potentially skilled as a manager than an American, a Japanese, a Frenchman, an Indian, or a Briton, but through no fault of his own he got off to a very late start. To develop his latent abilities calls for patience, understanding, humor, flexibility, and—most significantly—a readiness at all times to deal with African personnel as human beings, not as children or specially privileged individuals but as *fellow members* of a team. To be sure, all this is easier said than done, but the manager who recognizes and utilizes the African's potential will reap substantial growth dividends for both the local company and the parent organization.

Senior staff. During Pfizer's early years in Africa, it was policy to send senior African staff members to England for periods of training lasting from three to six months. The system, however, proved less than ideal, as the trainee, upon returning home, tended to leave the company and enter government service. This posed a particular problem in Ghana, where a local idiom describes the individual with an overseas education as "Mr. Been To." (He has, of course, "been to" the United States or Europe.) Since a distinct status attaches to the expression, a "Mr. Been To" often loses his sense of proportion; if he remains in the company, he frequently demands expensive cars and housing, as well as a higher salary than his training and responsibilities warrant. Unfortunately, this loss of perspective is also, in many instances, accompanied by a falling-off in efficiency. Indeed, Pfizer rapidly found that the performance of overseas-trained African staff members proved so often to be inferior to that of colleagues with local education that it was impossible to escape the conclusion that management qualifications do not necessarily require foreign training. Today, potential managers like the Ghanaian sales manager mentioned previously are sent overseas only after serving with the company for a considerable period of time. Basic training for management candidates is conducted within the African area.

Junior staff. Generally speaking, Africans and particularly Ghanaians available for clerical positions are of high caliber and speak good English. Women are starting to go into office jobs in increasing numbers, but our experience has shown that men, for the present at least, are preferable. In most African societies, equal status with men—and therefore education— is not encouraged among women, and although there is in Ghana a remarkable class of female entrepreneur which virtually controls the highly lucrative outdoor market economy of Accra, few women are yet qualified by training to work in Western business offices.

The normal terms of service for junior employees are:

- A trial period of three months, with the right on either side to terminate the contract within 14 days. After this initial period, termination is extended to four weeks.
- Free medical service. This has recently been replaced by the introduction of a medical scheme in which the employees can participate.
- Leave: 14 working days per year.
- Sick leave: Payable up to three months according to the manager's evaluation of the individual case.
- Salary: $80 to $140 per month for junior office employees; $30 to $50 per month for manual employees.

* * *

Pfizer's journey along the road to growth in Ghana has not been a smooth ride on a well-paved highway. Instead, it has been marked by countless detours and inaccurate road maps, not to mention driver error. The same roadblocks are being encountered by Pfizer organizations elsewhere in Africa, and at times we may even have been tempted to ask ourselves, "Is this trip really necessary?" The answer can only be in the affirmative. Indeed, we are convinced that the trip is not merely necessary but eminently desirable. Our growth in Africa, if not spectacular, has been steady. As we continue to do business with the continent's young nations, we continue to come to terms with the difficulties arising from their often unique needs. Much remains to be learned, and we will probably never learn it all. Yet, with a steadily expanding market and a corresponding increase in volume, the outlook on our future in Africa cannot be considered as other than optimistic. To put it in material terms, if we did not see long-range substantial earnings accruing from our African investment, we would not be in Africa. In addition, we are helping the African people, in a very practical way, to realize their "revolution of rising expectations."

GENERAL FOODS ACTIVITIES IN CENTRAL AFRICA •

PIERRE BEURSKENS

A FEW YEARS AGO the mention of Central Africa in business circles of the United States would have brought nothing except questioning looks. Few Americans knew anything about this vast area, the so-called Dark Continent, with its millions of people and its amazing diversities of terrain and culture. The countries of Central Africa were the special preserve of France and Britain who—although accomplishing some good in public works and education—administered their territories primarily for the exploitation of natural resources.

Now, however, most of us are aware of the dramatic turn of events that has brought political independence to these nations and made them a new force in international affairs. At least, we are aware that they exist because we hear about the importance of their votes in the United Nations, of the economic aid they frequently seek from us, and of their political upheavals and changes of government. Still, I suspect that many have but scant knowledge of the area and would be unable to recall very many facts and figures about such nations as Dahomey, Chad, Mali, and Upper Volta.

The area of West Africa includes 18 countries from the southern reaches of the Sahara to the lush equatorial rain forests. The countries of East Africa include such nations as Sudan, Ethiopia, Uganda, Tanzania, and Kenya. The 18 nations are Mauritania, Mali, Senegal, Gambia, Guinea, Sierra Leone, Liberia, Ivory Coast, Upper Volta, Ghana, Togo,

PIERRE BEURSKENS is Manager, Export-Sales—Europe, Africa, Asia & Pacific, General Foods Corporation, White Plains, New York.

Dahomey, Niger, Nigeria, Chad, Cameroun, the Central African Republic, and Gabon. These countries vary greatly in size, from Chad with an area of approximately 495,000 square miles (about the combined size of Texas, Colorado, and Wyoming) to Gambia which is the smallest nation in Africa with approximately 4,000 square miles. Populations range from approximately 7.5 million in Ghana to only 450,000 in Gabon. Illiteracy rates run from about 75 percent in Ghana up to 90 percent or more in several countries. Per capita annual income—and this is based on sketchy statistics available from 1962—ranges from about $60 in Mauritania to about $200 in Ghana. This can be compared to the United States figure for the same period of $2,242.

It is not surprising that this group of nations has been one of the areas of the world relatively untouched by international commerce of the United States. Certainly, the area does not appear—even today—to offer exceedingly attractive markets. Purchasing power is extremely low; illiteracy reduces the possibilities for advertising and promoting products; distribution is complicated by the lack of adequate transportation facilities. In addition, many of the emerging nations of Central Africa have shaky political situations. Within recent months, there have been political upheavals in Dahomey, the Central African Republic, Upper Volta, the Congo, Nigeria, Ghana, and Uganda. *The New York Times,* in an editorial on military coups in Dahomey, the Central African Republic, and Upper Volta, attributed them to "unemployment, low wages, inflation, a swollen and corrupt bureaucracy, unpopular government austerity and antigraft measures, and political unrest apparently exploited by agents of Communist China."

Prospects for developing viable and prosperous economies in these three countries, according to *The New York Times,* are slight unless the nations work toward building economic cooperation with their neighbors. So far, such economic agreements and compacts have been relatively ineffective in Central Africa. This would seem to argue strongly against Central Africa as a possible market for the products of United States manufacturers.

However, there is an equally strong argument in favor of looking at the world's underdeveloped nations—in Africa, Asia, and South America—as the markets of the future. The great bulk of our foreign commerce today is, of course, conducted with the developed nations of the world. But these nations occupy a small part of the earth's surface and contain but a small part of the earth's population. Many of these nations are themselves growing economically, and some are beginning to coordinate their economies in associations such as the European Common Market. As a result, U.S.

goods face increasing competition in international markets; and while the United States is still a dominant economic force in the world, it is not as dominant as it was at the end of World War II.

This points up the desirability of creating new markets in the under-developed nations. We may well find that the best and most efficient way of boosting the economies of these nations is to discover their urgent needs and to stimulate demand for new products. Even a small increase in trade with an underdeveloped country could have a major effect upon that nation's economy. Thus the real need in these nations is a creative market-ing effort, which may prove to be the most significant and permanent con-tribution that the United States could make to world economic develop-ment.

General Foods has long been engaged in international trade. However, until recently, the major area in which it had not established any efficient sales network was the emerging nations of Central Africa. In January 1963 I was assigned by the company's International Division to undertake a marketing campaign in this area. My first step was to read everything available on selling in Africa, and it did not take me long to discover that there was little literature of value on this subject. At the same time, I visited the New York offices of some of the large African trading companies. Since I did not receive as much assistance as I would have liked at these offices, I went on to the head offices in London and Paris before beginning a slow and careful journey through the nations of Central Africa.

In determining the potential of any foreign market there are some basics that must be examined. Among these are population, income, literacy, social and cultural factors, transportation, climate, natural resources, monetary exchange, and the political climate. It was soon apparent that reliable statistics and facts on many of these items did not exist for some of the Central African nations. Figures varied from source to source even on such things as the area of a country. Population figures were, in some cases, little more than educated guesses, as were figures on per capita income. There was little or nothing on income distribution, and it is here that developing nations present a special problem since there is often great variance between income in the cities and in the agricultural sections of a country. Social, cultural, and religious factors are important—particular-ly to a food company—because they sometimes determine what products may be eaten as well as influence advertising and packaging.

General Foods allowed me a great deal of freedom while on the tour of Africa. Very few decisions had to be cleared through the home office, and I was able to make quick judgments or to postpone decisions when it appeared advisable. There was an adequate budget for launching on-the-spot advertising or giveaway campaigns.

One thing which I discovered very quickly was that the French trading companies are primarily interested in protecting their markets and are closely controlled from Paris. They will not handle goods which are not sold in France, and they have a virtual stranglehold on the retail stores in the former French colonies. These markets are actually more French than France. For example, all packaging and promotional material must be completely in French. Despite fears that dealing with a trading company would cut off General Foods from other marketing channels, I decided that the only route to markets like Senegal and the Ivory Coast lay through a French trading company.

The Ivory Coast is one of the wealthiest of all the former French colonies in Africa. By African standards, it is a rich nation; by world standards, it is also a nation with great potential. However, 95 percent of the wealth of the country is derived from agriculture, and its major exports are agricultural products. The key crop is coffee, of which it is the world's third largest producer, trailing only Brazil and Colombia. Other exports include cocoa and wood, primarily mahogany and iroko. The structure of foreign trade is strong. In 1963, for example, total imports were $171.8 million; total exports were $227.8 million, giving a favorable balance of about $56 million.

The Ivory Coast has an area of about 124,000 square miles (somewhat larger than Arizona) and a population currently estimated at 3,750,-000. It became an independent nation in 1960 and, although remaining outside the French community, has signed a bilateral agreement retaining close ties with France. The president, Félix Houphouët-Boigny, is one of the ablest leaders in Africa. He has been in the forefront of the movement to encourage economic and political coordination between the new nations.

Senegal, which surrounds the tiny nation of Gambia on three sides, has been through centuries of westernization, and the Senegalese gained French citizenship in 1848, roughly 100 years before Africans in other French territories were granted citizenship rights. Senegal is one of the most highly industrialized of the African nations, with soap factories and oil mills which process a large part of its major crop, peanuts. There are also a sugar refinery, several food-processing plants, three textile mills, and several chemical plants. Major exports are agricultural and mineral products. In 1963 imports totaled about $166 million, while exports were $140 million.

Senegal has an area of approximately 77,000 square miles (about the size of South Dakota) and a population currently estimated at 3,400,000. It, too, became an independent nation in 1960 but retains extremely close ties with France. The president, Léopold Senghor, is one of the outstanding intellectuals of Africa. He won fame as a French poet long before he became a political leader.

Access to these two potentially rich markets was vitally important. However, it required an entire year—and three visits to Paris—before I was able to induce a French trading company to introduce one General Foods product in one market. Anyone can understand, therefore, why we have delayed further efforts to make arrangements in other markets of ex-French Africa until we have firmly cemented our ties with this trading company.

A quite different situation exists in the ex-British countries of West Africa: Ghana, Nigeria, and Sierra Leone.

Ghana, formerly the Gold Coast, was the pioneer for independence of the West African nations. Since gaining independence in 1957, Ghana has become one of the richest and most progressive of the former colonies. Its per capita annual income is approximately $200—a figure that many economists use to distinguish between a developed and underdeveloped nation. The chief source of wealth lies in cocoa, of which it is the world's largest producer. In 1963 Ghana's imports totalled £132 million, while exports were approximately £104 million.

Ghana has an area of almost 92,000 square miles (about the size of Oregon) and a population currently estimated at 7,500,000. In contrast to other emerging African nations, Ghana had a large corps of educated native leaders ready to take over when independence was granted.

Unfortunately, because of President Kwame Nkrumah's personal aspirations, the economy has seriously deteriorated during the last few years. His overthrow seems to have restored confidence in this country's ability to rise from its current economic plight.

Nigeria is one of the most fascinating countries in Africa. It is the twelfth most populous nation in the world, and the most densely populated large nation in Africa. Current sources estimate its population as high as 56 million. However, Wattenberg and Smith in their book, *The New Nations of Africa,* placed the 1960 population at only 36 million. The country is largely nonindustrial, and the average annual income is less than $90. Natural resources represent Nigeria's greatest potential. Its production of tin ore, for example, reached 1.5 million tons in 1960. It has the only coal deposits in West Africa, and recent explorations have revealed substantial oil reserves.

Sierra Leone, the smallest of the three nations, has an area of about 28,000 square miles (approximately the size of South Carolina). It, too, is one of the less developed nations of West Africa. Undoubtedly, the climate has much to do with this, because it is extremely hot and humid. Freetown, the capital, has a mean daily temperature of 81 degrees and receives more than 150 inches of rainfall per year. Nonetheless, the country would seem to have a promising future. There are important mineral resources, including diamonds, and a diversity of flourishing cash crops, including palm oil, coffee, and cocoa. The country has a very small import-export deficit.

Ghana, Nigeria, and Sierra Leone can be approached individually or as a unit through one of the large international trading companies. While the British trading companies do stress goods made in the United Kingdom, they are much less rigidly controlled from the head office than their French counterparts. Local managers can usually get their London offices to purchase any goods which will increase profits.

The other basic difference between these markets and those of ex-French Africa is the availability of good alternative wholesaling and retailing channels. Since a tie-in with a trading company is normally exclusive, I sought a representative of British nationality who could handle all three markets. He acts as a commission agent for large customers and an importer-distributor for smaller ones; his staff is almost entirely African; he has warehouses and vans; and his financial position merits 60-day collection credit. In addition, the representative was able to arrange for competitive trading company retail stores to carry General Foods products. An advertising campaign did not seem to be called for at the time these arrangements were made; we did supply point-of-sale material.

Still another approach was used in Liberia, where GF products were already being sold through Firestone plantation stores and by local retailers via New York wholesale exporters. A radio advertising program was begun immediately, and a Lebanese merchant who runs the largest retail outlet in the capital, Monrovia, was selected as a representative. This firm imports its own needs and sells to wholesalers and other retailers on a commission basis and out of its own stock. As a result of these arrangements, sales doubled within seven months.

Still other approaches were used in East Africa—Kenya, Uganda, Tanzania, and Ethiopia—with equally good or better results, and GF now has a solid African marketing network. Distribution channels have been clearly established with special attention to particular local conditions. In time, other African markets will also be approached.

The major lesson learned from this campaign was the necessity for complete flexibility of approach. Using the same sales route into every market affords simplicity and ease of control, but maximum sales depend upon a distribution system tailored to each market. In one country a local importer-distributor may be best. In another, it may be a commission representative arranging sales with various buyers, or an importer-retailer acting as a distributor. In some cases a firm's own sales company might be best.

Other important pointers for selling the African markets are as follows:

- Individual distribution, credit, and advertising methods are essential for each country, although a few countries can sometimes be treated as one unit. There is a wide range of size and sophistication between African markets.
- Spending habits are heavily influenced by white-expatriate purchasing patterns; initial sales attempts should be made in shops frequented by expatriates.
- A path has already been cleared in some markets by foreign subsidiaries and licensees (particularly from South Africa), U.S. wholesale exporters, and foreign trading companies; a campaign may be built on these inroads.
- Native distributors or representatives are seldom capable of handling a foreign firm's goods; but whatever the nationality of the local distributor, his staff should be largely Africanized, that is, made up almost entirely of local nationals.
- Sales can be boosted mightily just by visits and encouragement from the home company. Quick advertising pays off handsomely where the goods are already available.
- The ideal representative for nondurables is an agent selling on a commission basis to large wholesalers, who also has enough financial resources to import for his own account and thus service the many small traders who cannot buy direct. Unfortunately, few such agents exist.
- Some product lines are best sourced from subsidiaries in countries that have been supplying the African markets in the past, for reasons of familiarity and various tariff preferences (particularly in ex-French areas), but U.S.-made goods can be successfully phased in with time.

AN AMERICAN ENTERPRISE IN
EMERGING AFRICA •

J. C. DEAN

OUR COMPANY has been doing business in most of Africa for over half a century. It was, in fact, one of the first oil companies to begin trading on the west coast in the early 1900's. I personally am optimistic about Africa's future and believe that prospects there are good for American business.

Our company's overseas operations are grouped into geographical "regions," and I am responsible for the region we officially call Mediterranean and Africa. Our region encompasses 66 countries and territories, nearly half of which achieved independence in the past ten years. In North, West, and East Africa, we have operations in 34 countries that are full-fledged members of the United Nations. Also, our affiliates do business in some 15 other locations in Africa that are still under colonial rule. All of these countries or territories are in the "developing," or if you prefer, the "emerging" stage.

In some countries we are exploring for oil; in others we have found it and are producing and transporting it to world markets; in still others we are refining it. And in all of them we are selling finished products. In a few countries we perform all of these functions.

Many of our problems are the same as those that confront the international oil business in other parts of the world, especially where we are exploring, producing, or refining. In Africa, however, we face a wider range of management problems that cut across all functions of our busi-

J. C. DEAN is President, Mobil Mediterranean and Africa Inc., Paris, France.

ness. These are the problems we shall concentrate on here—with special emphasis on our marketing operations south of the Sahara. Here our company is most often the leading American commercial enterprise on the local scene.

The first problem, in general terms, arises because of the size and diversity of Africa. Here is the world's second largest land mass, into which you could easily fit Red China and the United States and still have room left over for Europe. The 250 million people who live in Africa are as varied as those to be found on any other continent. Most of them are dirt poor; a few, fabulously rich. They speak some 700 languages and have created political systems that run the gamut from feudal monarchies to socialist republics. Africa is certainly a continent of contrast and contradiction.

It's risky for anyone to generalize about Africa. But it is especially dangerous for businessmen, because Africa is too big, too varied, and too restless to be wrapped up in neat generalities. The only sensible approach is to look at individual countries in Africa as separate and distinct areas for doing business.

There are the basic problems of climate, disease, and pests. Most of Africa south of the Sahara is hot and humid, day after day, month after month, year after year. The continent is plagued by most of the diseases and pests known to mankind. Many of our customers, and our employees as well, are exposed to such tropical diseases as malaria, sleeping sickness, parasite worms, and yellow fever. In many areas climate and disease account for an indifferent approach toward work. This is a tough management problem, because one obviously can't air-condition a continent. If you stay in Africa long enough, you stand a good chance of coming down with a sort of lassitude. Little things begin going wrong with your work. Appointments don't really seem important. Nothing actually *has* to be done right away. I realize that this malady is not restricted to Africa—I've seen plenty of cases in New York and elsewhere—but the incidence rate is definitely much higher in Africa.

Unstable politics are another problem. We are all familiar with the series of political crises that have erupted in Africa in 1965 and 1966. A prominent African businessman gave me his own explanation for Africa's persistent political malaise. He felt that independence came too suddenly and too easily to the world's poorest, most ill-prepared countries. This is a strong statement, but it begins to make sense when we examine the legacy of colonialism.

It is quite clear that the cause of some of Africa's current troubles lies with its former colonial rulers. Although some of the colonial powers had fairly enlightened policies, others did not. In many places, "divide and rule" was the watchword. By dividing, the colonial powers repressed the development of political conditions that lead to effective government institutions. Arbitrary and artificial boundaries were drawn up and imposed. These so-called national boundaries split up many of Africa's major tribes and helped produce the balkanization that exists today.

In addition, only a thin rank of African civil servants or technologists were trained by the colonial powers, who used their own nationals instead. When freedom came to the Congo, for example, there were among the Africans no doctors, one lawyer, a mere 31 university graduates, and only 84 junior high school teachers.

What does this mean to a company trying to do business in these countries? It means that some of the government officials it deals with often do not have the experience needed to work smoothly with businessmen. It means that the company often gets tangled up with bureaucracy at its worst. Incidentally, doing business in Africa inevitably entails being intimately involved with government on every level. The government is one's partner, not only when a new investment is being negotiated but on a day-to-day basis thereafter. Our managers spend countless hours with government officials, sometimes over simple requests. Approval from half a dozen ministers, the vice president, and often the president himself is needed in many places for such simple things as obtaining a service station site, building a house, or remitting a dividend.

Getting information from the government is equally frustrating and time consuming. Often the information one desperately needs for planning or accounting purposes just doesn't exist. There are few people in the new governments equipped to prepare demand forecasts or any other statistical information that is handed out regularly by governments in developed countries. If the information does exist, there is always a long wait before it is made available. Furthermore, the turnover rate in African ministries is extremely high; and if one of the key people is away on a trip, one might as well relax—sometimes for a month or two.

One point to keep in mind is that in many of the newer countries the concept of private enterprise on any scale larger than that of the old river trader has no really established tradition. Even worse, private enterprise usually clashes with the political outlook of many politicians in Africa. Many of them have been trained (in England, France, and even in the United States) to believe that the state is the only proper source from which to secure the funds needed for investment. They misinterpret the motives of companies such as ours. They are afraid of economic domination from outside. This is why, for example, some African governments insist on participation in ventures that are usually handled by private enterprise in other countries.

Many government officials are not at all convinced that private initiative is the key to progress. Even if they are neutral in attitude toward private enterprise, they feel that they haven't got time to adopt this road toward economic development. Some of them have preferred the short-cut methods of the Soviets or the Chinese. This helps explain the inconsistency often found in some countries, where private enterprise is encouraged with one hand and socialist controls are adopted with the other.

Africa's lack of familiarity with private enterprise is a crucial management problem. However, it is being encountered less and less. Since 1965 there has been a definite change in the attitudes of several African leaders when their experience with American business has been favorable. I cannot emphasize too strongly that a company should be completely frank and open in its dealings with African government officials. The more they know about a business and the role it plays in their society, the less suspicion and hostility they are likely to display.

One will, of course, occasionally run across an official who is corrupt and open to bribery. This should come as no surprise, for such individuals are found in every government. How does a manager deal with this problem? As far as we are concerned, the answer is easy. We stand firm in refusing to buy our way into a country, a business deal, or anything else. Our people realize that bribery is morally wrong and politically dangerous. Some others have not had the same compunctions, but they are finding out that they are now subject to blackmail for the foreseeable future, with no easy escape.

Turning to economic problems of doing business in Africa, we find that more than 90 percent of Africa's 250 million people are engaged in subsistence farming. They are poorly clothed, poorly housed, and poorly fed. Of the world's annual production of goods and services, Africa accounts for only about 2 percent of the total value. Per capita income, excluding South Africa, is less than $100 a year. Vulnerable, one-crop economies are the rule rather than the exception.

Communications are erratic, both to Europe and especially between African states. A cable from Accra to Abidjan (less than an hour away by plane) generally goes to London, where it is sent to Paris and then relayed to Abidjan, arriving three or four days after it was sent.

Transportation in Africa is equally deficient. Waterways and railways are the chief forms of transport. Good hard-topped or even gravel roads are few and far between in tropical areas. Most roads are dirt, with many stretches washed out in the rainy season. Air travel has helped to a certain extent. But the lack of adequate transportation is one of the main obstacles to development in Africa.

These are basic economic difficulties, which perhaps can be solved with money and determination. The tougher problem we encounter is the lack of economic understanding about business operations in general, which results in suspicion and distrust. Our company has found that it takes more than just sound engineering and modern equipment to complete a successful venture in Africa. This is especially true when we are in an area where nobody understands what we are doing and where many people are ready to believe the worst about foreigners.

Success for these projects lies in creating basic understanding, a requirement that doesn't always exist elsewhere. But this is easier said than done. One can't take a full-page advertisement in the local paper when operating in a tropical jungle or in a remote area of the desert. First, there is usually no paper; second, even if there were, only a few people in the village or oasis could read it. Yet one must dispel suspicion and distrust wherever they exist if one is to get the job done.

In contrast to the lack of economic understanding in the bush, the African trade union movement is economically sophisticated and strong in many urban centers. Of course, in some countries trade unions do not exist at all or are suppressed by the regimes in power. However, it is true that unions are growing in strength and number in many countries. Witness the general strikes experienced in Nigeria in 1964—they paralyzed the entire nation.

In the absence of a strong middle class, the trade unions play a major role in the economy. They take a firm stand on most political issues and have produced many important nationalist leaders. Vigorous union activity is, of course, nothing new to experienced managers. What makes union power a special problem in some parts of Africa, however, is that there are often no countervailing forces to temper labor's demands.

Thus far I have been discussing the larger economic and political problems confronting our managers in Africa. But management itself presents a very real problem in our operations. I am referring to the problems of staffing, development, and Africanization. In our African marketing affiliates, we employ 4,600 people, of whom only about 220 are foreign nationals. Actually, we have two sets of problems: the ones presented by our foreigners and the ones presented by local nationals.

Many Europeans joined our company prior to the independence of countries in which they work, some of them expecting to make a career of service in Africa. Although today's working and living conditions which we provide are good, life just isn't the same for these people. Professionally and psychologically the pressures have increased a great deal since colonial days. Some foreigners, including some Americans, refuse to accept the fact that Africa is now independent. There are few places left for people with a "colonial mentality," and we are faced with the problem of weeding these people out.

The strong tide of Africanization leads some foreigners to realize that they are working themselves out of a job. Those with good potential are no problem—they can work for us in other countries throughout the world. Others, however, who are doing good jobs but have limited potential, are unhappy and worried about their future. They are dissatisfied and, as a result, show little incentive for developing plans and programs to solve the tough problems confronting the company.

Recruiting new people is becoming much more difficult. Things are good in Europe; they are not so good south of the Mediterranean. The uncertainty over Africa's future and the future of the white man there puts off many good candidates. Nevertheless, because of the severity of the problems we face, we need the very best people we can get.

Africa is an excellent training ground for young executives. The problems described earlier are not easily solved; but by working at them, a man becomes highly qualified in a hurry, because he has to if he is to get the job done. Also, there is no limit placed on his abilities or talents. And this is the kind of person our company (and industry in general) will need in the developing countries for a long, long time to come.

Despite this need, any foreign investor's future in Africa depends largely on the training and development of local nationals to fill executive jobs. This is what the governments want. This is what the unions want. And this is what we want—strictly from a dollars-and-cents point of view.

But Africanization is a slow process, even though we know we are working against the clock. In some countries, we have made excellent progress. In Ghana, for example, our affiliate has only 12 foreign nationals in a work force of 360. Many of our top management spots are occupied by Ghanaians. In other countries our progress to date has not been equally satisfactory. Frankly, the problems presented by Africanization are enormous. They demand a calm disposition, a willingness to spend money without getting a fast return, and, above all, infinite patience—qualities that are not found in all managers.

For a wide variety of reasons, many Africans do not regard economic activity as an especially desirable goal in itself. Only recently have some individuals become involved in the money economy. For generations, the great majority worked only long enough to obtain food, clothing, and shelter. Tribal traditions, social taboos, and religious training established other values for the individual.

Most Africans today participate actively in elaborate social, political, and religious life of their tribe and village. If an African works in a city, his ties with his village are still strong, and he returns whenever he can. These are the traditional noneconomic activities he enjoys, and work is simply not as important to him. In many African societies a man has always worked only when he felt like it and stopped when he felt like it. (Who is to say there is anything wrong with this approach to life?)

Those few Africans who do exist on better than subsistence levels generally have this same attitude. They are interested more in spending than in saving and investing. Some African leaders unfortunately have set the example in this regard with multimillion-dollar palaces, elaborate airports, and fancy hotels. The accumulation of capital for investment in productive enterprise is not so popular a concept, except in a few places such as Nigeria where private capital has developed.

Once hired, it takes the average African a considerable time to acquire a disciplined loyalty to his job. Many times a worker is surprisingly quick to learn a particular skill, but this may be because of his capacity for imitation. He may not at all understand why he is doing what he does or what relationship his job has to the next man's job.

At the same time, however, an African worker is a man to be reckoned with. His government wants us to train him. His union insists that he work and that he be promoted. He often has relatives in the government who back him to the hilt. However unsuited he may be to employment, he is a citizen of the host country as well as our employee. The judgments he forms of our conduct may in the long run determine the success or failure of our operations in his country. It's just that simple, so we are patient. We spend a lot of time training him, and we try to encourage him to become interested in productive economic activity.

Unfortunately, once he is trained and producing at a reasonable level, the chances are he will be invited to work for the government. Our company is an excellent springboard for government service. One prominent government official now advertises on his official calling card the fact that he is a former employee of ours.

Even Africans educated in Europe and the United States are more interested in politics, government service, and the liberal professions than they are in running their own business or working for a private concern. They want to see their country develop economically, but by and large they want to plan or administer this development. They are not as eager to be risk-takers or day-to-day managers.

This explains our problem of "absentee dealers" in many countries in Africa. An individual with enough money to buy and resell petroleum products usually doesn't want to "degrade" himself by spending time at his service station. He isn't interested in working for better service, or higher sales, or improved station housekeeping; he turns the actual running of the station over to a relative or friend.

Yet without strong and widespread personal commitment and drive, African enterprise can't develop on a large scale. This is a serious problem because, in the long term, the future of these developing nations will be determined by the kind and extent of economic activities which the Africans themselves are willing and able to undertake.

At this point the question may arise: "What is your company doing in Africa anyway?" The only answer I can give is that we believe in Africa's future. I say *Africa's* future, fully recognizing that some of the smaller countries that are the product of colonial fragmentation may never become economically viable until they unite. But certainly the larger countries do have a future, and we want to share in it. In the last half century, or longer in some cases, we have enjoyed profitable operations in Africa, and we think we have made a real contribution to our host countries as well. Today we are faced with new problems and vexations, but these will diminish as the new Africa gets its house in order.

So much for some of the problems of doing business in Africa. We could spend much more time listing the opportunities that Africa potentially holds out to the intelligent foreign investor. I am not alone in my optimism. Many companies have entered Africa since independence. The managers of these companies know that in some areas there may still be some sliding back for a few years, but they also know that the economic surge forward *will* come; and when it does, they want to be ready.

Not too long ago I read an article about the formative years of a newly independent country. The actions of the government were typical. Many opposition leaders were booted out into a neighboring colony. Those who remained were persecuted, thrown in jail, and had their property expropriated. The native tribes were oppressed, corruption flourished in high places, and the government refused to allow military bases on its soil. The government gobbled up foreign aid and credits, however, and condemned the greed of those who offered them. It applauded revolutions everywhere, while declaring its firm intention to stay neutral in the struggles between the great powers. Laws were passed making it a criminal offense to oppose measures of the government or to criticize the president. The weak opposition party protested that a one-party state was being created and that political freedom was dead.

This article could have been written about one of several African countries in 1966. But, in fact, it was describing conditions in the United States of America in 1790!

Practically all of the new nations of Africa are less than half a dozen years old. Granted they are making some mistakes and have a lot more debits on the ledger than the United States had when it started, but this is not the full story. At times there appear to me to be two separate and distinct Africas. One is the Africa of the headlines one reads: the exploding Africa of coups, revolutions, rigged elections, army mutinies, racial conflict, and anti-Western demonstrations. The other is the one seen on my rather frequent trips to Africa. This is the Africa of peaceful change and steady progress toward modernization, the Africa most people hear or read very little about. This is the Africa that in my estimation will persevere and endure. My estimate is based on hard facts that we have observed in recent years.

Africa is a rich continent, and it has enough natural resources to support economic growth. Except for Egypt, population pressure is not a matter of desperate and immediate concern, as it is in other developing areas. There is a real hunger and demand for education everywhere one turns in Africa, and mass elementary education is growing fast in most countries. The number of secondary schools, colleges, and universities also is increasing. Active road building programs are under way in many countries, and this factor alone is sure to contribute to more rapid economic development. Efforts are being made to stamp out disease by improving living conditions, health precautions, diets, and water purity.

It also is clear that past patterns of trade and production are being radically altered. New urban communities are coming into being. Large-scale mining, industrial, and agricultural projects are reaching completion in many of the countries. Purchasing power is rising. Some of these countries now realize that rapid progress cannot be produced by the magic wand of political independence. More and more African leaders are telling their people to work harder for economic development. Newly drafted five-year, six-year, and ten-year plans have been stretching out the unrealistic economic goals previously set.

Any investor interested in Africa would do well to examine these development plans carefully. While some of them may be drafted on shaky assumptions, nearly all of them outline the ways in which capital, labor, foreign exchange, and so forth will be allocated in the years ahead. Often the plans describe specific projects where foreign participation is needed to achieve certain planned objectives.

We also must recall that financial aid and technical assistance continue to pour into Africa from abroad. France, the United States, Great Britain, and West Germany are the big contributors, but the Russians and Chinese have helped out too. International organizations and private groups also are interested in African economic development. This assistance is taking hold in many countries. Already, we can see its impact in rising production and greater exports from Africa.

In addition, there seems to be a slow but steady increase in the number of regional economic organizations. If this healthy trend continues, it will surely help the smaller African nations to get on the road to economic viability. And despite the troubles encountered at its recent meetings, the Organization of African Unity still gives promise of becoming an effective vehicle for political and economic cooperation.

These are only a few of the factors that point to a good future for Africa once its vast potential is tapped and present political risks subside. In fact, some observers look at Africa—of all the developing areas of the world—as *theoretically* the place in which real economic, social, and even political progress is most likely. When this progress takes place, and it may not be as far off as we think, American business should be in a position to capitalize on new opportunities for investment.

BUSINESS CONDITIONS IN EAST AFRICA •

H. W. MANVILLE

AN INDICATOR OF THE INCREASED CONFIDENCE in doing business in East Africa, and in Kenya more particularly, is the fact that there was an increase from 20 U.S. businesses with direct representation in 1962 to 50 businesses in 1965. U.S. investment in Kenya may well be in the region of $90 million (U.S. dollars). With few exceptions these companies have good to excellent annual earnings, and nearly all have exceptional growth rates.

It was in 1931 that our company was first registered in East Africa, which comprises the countries of Kenya, Uganda, and Tanzania (formerly Tanganyika and Zanzibar). Nairobi, the capital of Kenya, was selected as the most suitable center. A retail store and administration offices were established, and for the next 25 years representation was built on the basis of distributors. Practically all the retail trading at this time was in the hands of the Asian community, as they were the purchasers of the produce from the Africans and in turn supplied them with their modest needs.

While this method of importing and wholesaling was both relatively uncomplicated and profitable, it had little growth potential; by 1956 our company had only a 45 percent share of the market against Japanese, German, and Italian competition. The difficulty lay in reaching the end user.

The end user, one of a population of 9 million in Kenya, 8 million in Uganda, and 10 million in Tanzania, was, as a volume purchaser of consumer durables, the African. It was to meet his needs that we needed to

H. W. MANVILLE is Vice President, Africa and Near East Division, Singer Sewing Machine Company, New York, New York.

align our marketing structure while still providing for the relatively quality market of wealthier Asians and Europeans, who numbered less than 2 percent of the total population.

The first basic need in retailing sewing machines is to teach the end user (1) why he needs the product and (2) the benefits it will bring once the acquisition has been made. To this end, we expanded our normal sales activity to include an educational program to teach women machine sewing; and from our students interest and sales began to flow. Trained women, themselves, started to train others.

The per capita income is extremely low, and it was quite impossible to sell a $150 item in volume for cash. Therefore, we moved toward hire purchase in a substantial way.

The market divided two ways. On the one hand, there was the domestic user who acquired a machine for home use and who represented a relatively small portion of the total users. Then there was the artisan, dressmaker, or tailor who set himself up in business and who proved to be the volume purchaser.

By steps we began to build a direct selling organization of commissioned sales agents, who worked out of small shops or depots, canvassing for sales. Having acquired a customer and closed a sale, thereafter the agent became the collector on that account, calling back monthly on the customer to see he still held the merchandise and that it was working satisfactorily, and to collect the payment.

All of these agents were Africans, with the exception of a very few Asians in senior positions. They became adept at assessing their customers' worth and moved freely in and out of homes, shops, offices, and the markets, acquiring their contacts. As we grew and gained confidence in our asset control, our terms were eased and payment periods extended. Repossessions on bad accounts were not too difficult, and repossessed merchandise was readily renovated and profitably resold.

Every new sale was carefully documented and controls introduced or increased as and when difficulties arose. Many a purchaser previously unemployed was able to get into his own business by raising the down payment and paying off installments with revenues earned from his tailoring activities. This type of cottage industry was widely welcomed by governments with vast unemployment situations.

The African tends to drift to urban centers for employment and then when planting or harvest time comes around will return to his native village. This presented a problem in keeping track of customers on the move. For every sale, through guarantors, references, and relatives, approximately

12 names and addresses were taken and, invariably, by persistence the customer could be traced.

Tracing needed coverage, and fairly soon we moved toward opening additional shops in major towns. As the volume of open accounts increased in each town, the shop was divided and another shop opened until some 120 shops have now been reached throughout East Africa.

We learned that the African is quite a born salesman but that one must sustain training over a long period. Furthermore, close supervision on matters covering control of cash and inventory had to be maintained. To keep contact with customers over an ever widening area, the transport fleet had to grow. Roads are rough and often impassable, distances are great, and transportation assumes major proportions in such a marketing structure, where a continual call back must be made. Included also in this sector is the relatively high cost of maintaining overseas personnel and of their travel on rotational vacation as well as within their territories.

Service is all important, since this type of customer is not the most delicate user of such merchandise. Service has been a major contributor in keeping ahead of competition; and despite the cost of training and providing mechanical staff and carrying inventories of spares with all their administrative problems, such back-up is essential to maintaining one's product among a developing population.

Once the company was satisfied with its asset control and able to obtain the necessary financing, every opportunity lay ahead to extend terms further and reduce down payments and at the same time secure the margins required for the desired returns. With such a marketing structure the growth potential is only limited by the aims of the enterprise.

For the African salesman an incentive payment is desirable in order to obtain productivity in both selling and in collecting cash. And such incentive should be carried from the salesman up through his manager and area manager.

About this time, having established this marketing structure, we decided to launch out into other products such as home entertainment, floor care, and climate control products, refrigerators, cooking ranges, and knitting machines. The selfsame people already our customers for sewing machines, whose credit standing had already been judged, became suitable customers for a whole range of new lines. The wide range of other products enabled us in a fairly short period virtually to double our sales turnover.

By now the salesmen employed had increased to some 600 and the well-tried pattern of sales contests had been given a run. The results achieved were astounding and out of all proportion to the monetary value of the prizes. The prestige of being the top man was the driving force. Great care must be taken to view new business at such times, as enthusiasm can easily outstrip intelligence in accepting new credit risks.

This has described our Singer marketing structure and how it has grown to its present size. With the forthcoming split in the three territories' currency and for other, ethnic reasons, it has become desirable for us to administer each of the three territories separately, and beginning in 1967 management offices will function in each of the capitals. This particular splitting of the territories for governmental administration is unfortunate, particularly because of the constant jealousies which arise and the tendencies of late for one territory to prohibit the import of certain goods from another in the misguided thought that this will force industrialists to have three manufacturing facilities instead of one. However, the three territories are still cooperating through a Common Services Organization, and this is the means of administering the railways, post and telecommunications, income tax, customs, the University of East Africa, and some research organizations.

With a few exceptions there is a free flow of goods between these territories, and we have decided to set up our own manufacturing and assembly venture in Nairobi. It has been planned to obtain lumber and veneer locally and manufacture all our requirements for sewing machine furniture. And in the hope that certain tariff advantages will be gained, sewing machines will also be assembled locally.

There is already in existence a variety of U.S. business ventures representing direct investment as well as a whole multitude of U.S. commodities handled by local representatives and agents. Most of the directly represented firms have expansion plans that include additional investment and increased local manufacture, depending upon market requirements.

There is an Investment Guarantee Law, and the various governments appreciate the need for a favorable political climate to attract private industry. It has been made clear that a thriving private sector is welcome. The Foreign Investment Protection Law welcomes new investment under "approved status" and gives the right of full repatriation of capital and profit.

A degree of control of the enterprise with personnel from overseas is essential, and working permits are no great difficulty provided the person has qualities to contribute. As mentioned above, the cost of keeping such personnel is fairly high with housing, transportation, rotational vacation, education allowance, and so forth all to be provided. The climate and living conditions in Nairobi are really quite ideal when comparing foreign stations, but a wide sense of humor and stamina to overcome the sheer frustration of working with Africans—whose life approach is so different from that of Americans and Europeans—are prime requirements.

The labor movement has been active throughout the territories, and it is doubtful if any foreign enterprise has escaped unionization. Many labor leaders are only interested in trade unionism for its political advantages.

With a view to closer identity with the territories' political and economic aspirations, we decided, as mentioned above, on a manufacturing venture. It is to be hoped that tariff advantages will be obtained, and the main deciding factor here is not so much to attract investment but to strengthen the enterprise against competition. There is a growing distaste for foreign investment to be utilized in the retail trade, which is one of the easiest apparent ventures in which the local population can engage. Rather, foreign investment is welcomed more in industrial ventures providing local employment, and a contribution of technical know-how is practically essential.

The territories are, of course, still linked to the sterling area, and up to now 98 percent of the exchange control procedures guiding foreign investment have been handled in Nairobi. I will not attempt to describe any of the numerous regulations, but suffice it to say the governments have been fairly flexible and no difficulties have been encountered in repatriating profits.

Main exports from Kenya are coffee, sisal, and tea; from Uganda, cotton and coffee; and from Tanzania, sisal and cotton. Trade balances have been unfavorable for many years and budgets balanced by external aid, mainly from Britain. In Kenya a substantial land utilization change has been and still is taking place. Large farming areas formerly occupied by European farmers producing quality crops and livestock are now being parceled out in small lots to poor and inexperienced African farmers producing their own subsistence requirements and limited cash crops. In the short term this can only be detrimental to the economy, which is broadly based on agriculture.

The following is some general advice to U.S. firms interested in doing business in East Africa:

- A company can prosper if it will offer services and maintain adequate stocks of spares.
- Do not fear being priced out of the market—quality and durability still count in the cost.
- Approach the market with vigor, as halfhearted attempts can only meet with failure.

- Work the market, but do not use it as an area to take up slack when U.S. sales are low and neglect it when business improves.
- Be prepared to assist with credit, as businesses are small and limited in finance; they cannot afford to have capital tied up over a long period of time.
- Be prepared to meet local conditions halfway—the U.S. way may not be acceptable locally.
- Trade delegations can achieve success if they are ready to accept orders.
- Consider using mobile sales units, particularly in the country areas where more traditional forms of advertising are of little value.
- Avoid undue delay in processing orders and delivery.
- Safeguard quality on products partly or wholly manufactured locally and bearing U.S. brand names to be sure that they match up to U.S. quality standards.

The governments welcome inquiries, and investment opportunities range over a host of items, from toothbrushes and flashlight bulbs to garments and tractors. To repeat, the earnings range from good to excellent. Doing business in East Africa can be a somewhat frustrating experience but one that offers ample rewards.

SOUTH AFRICA: THE SCOPE FOR INVESTMENT AND GENERAL BUSINESS CONDITIONS •

ROY B. HILL

THE REPUBLIC OF SOUTH AFRICA lies in the rough triangle at the foot of the African continent formed by the Atlantic and Indian Oceans and the Limpopo River. The country consists of four provinces: the Cape of Good Hope, with an area of 278,465 square miles; Natal, 33,578 square miles; the Transvaal, 110,450 square miles; and the Orange Free State, 49,866 square miles. The total area of 472,359 square miles is but one-eighth of the total area of the United States. The High Commission territories of Basutoland, Bechuanaland, and Swaziland, although within South Africa's ethnic, geographical, and economic framework, do not form part of the Republic and are administered by the United Kingdom.

South Africa was first discovered by Portuguese explorers who rounded the Cape in the fifteenth century in the hope of discovering a sea route to the East. They reported the existence of small groups of nomadic people at the Cape—Bushmen and Hottentots. The Bushmen, who were at the Stone Age level of existence, lived on what they hunted or on wild roots and berries; the Hottentots, on the contrary, were a pastoral people.

Western civilization came to South Africa with the Dutch, who settled at the Cape in 1652. Jan van Riebeeck, leader of the settlers, was instructed by the Dutch East India Company to establish a provision station at Table Bay, to provide fresh food for the company's merchantmen on their voy-

---

ROY B. HILL is General Manager, Colgate-Palmolive Ltd., Boksburg, South Africa.

ages from Holland to the East Indies and back. The van Riebeeck settlement at the Cape was the nucleus from which white South Africa has grown.

Most of the white citizens of South Africa (approximately 4 million) are descended from the early Dutch, British, French, and German settlers. The nonwhite population can be divided into three main racial groups: the Bantu, who number 11 million; the Coloreds, 1.5 million; and the Asians, of whom there are .5 million. (These figures are based on 1961 statistics.)

The origin of the Bantu in South Africa can be traced back many centuries to when they migrated southward in three great streams from the vicinity of the Great Lakes in Central Africa. One group settled in Angola and the Congo basin, the second group settled in Bechuanaland and parts of the Transvaal, and the third group migrated into Natal and the Northern Cape Province. The Coloreds are chiefly descended from slaves introduced from the East in the days of the Dutch East India Company and from the Hottentots, now nearly extinct, with an infusion of white blood from European settlers. The Asian sector of the community is made up mostly of Indians who came to South Africa as indentured laborers on the sugar plantations of Natal. Their numbers were later supplemented by other Indians who came to the country on their own account, mostly as craftsmen, traders, and merchants.

Nearly one-half of the Bantu still live in Bantu territories, areas which belonged to their forefathers. Here they lead a simple, pastoral existence. A large number of Bantu have, however, been attracted by the lights and adventure of the cities, and they have found employment in industry and commerce, in a great variety of occupations which the virile economy of the country has to offer. These people, known as the "urbanized Bantu," have been strongly influenced by the white man's way of life and are no longer faithful to many of their tribal traditions. The third group of Bantu live on farms in the country, owned by white farmers, and are employed as agricultural laborers. Like their compatriots in the Bantu territories, they have retained many of their old customs and traditions.

The South African Government's policy is to encourage and assist the Bantu to develop their territories into self-governing national homelands. Decentralization of "white" territories and the establishment of industries in the border areas near the Bantu homelands, calculated to secure a more equitable distribution of wealth and contribute to the economic development of the homelands, are firm matters of Government policy. This policy will also insure employment for Bantu resident in their homelands and will eliminate the necessity for migrant labor in the border areas.

THE ECONOMY OF SOUTH AFRICA

South Africa's national income, after allowing for interest, dividends, and other payments abroad, rose from R1,386 million in 1946-47 to R5,070 million in 1962-63—an increase of 266 percent in 16 years. ("R" stands for "Rand," the basic monetary unit of South Africa.) Its growth rate since the war compares favorably with the rate of advance in the United States and the United Kingdom.

The average individual income in 1962-63 of approximately R300 is low in comparison with standards in America and the United Kingdom, because the inclusion of nonwhites, particularly those in the rural subsistence areas, depresses the average. Nevertheless, it is still well in excess of that of any other country on the African continent.

Secondary industry in South Africa has developed continuously and has become increasingly diversified and technologically advanced during the World War II and postwar years. The gold mining industry, a major consumer of industrial products, has stimulated this expansion and diversification of secondary industry. Today South Africa manufactures a wide range of consumer goods, such as foodstuffs, textiles and clothing, footwear, and metal products. Capital goods, including industrial and mining machinery and transport and electrical equipment, have also been manufactured on a considerable scale in recent years.

Among the industries that have grown since the war are the textile industry, which has grown remarkably, and the paper and pulp industry, which has likewise made great strides. The chemical industry has also expanded rapidly and is being given a significant stimulus through the by-products that have become available from SASOL (the oil-from-coal plant of the South African Coal, Oil and Gas Corporation). In response to Governmental encouragement aimed at increasing the locally made content of motor vehicles assembled in South Africa, the motor industry has likewise expanded and grown rapidly in recent years.

South Africa is fortunate in possessing vast resources of commercially exploitable mineral deposits. Apart from gold, uranium, and diamonds, more than 60 other base metals and minerals are mined, both for internal consumption by the iron and steel and other industries and for export on a large scale.

Although the output of the agricultural, forestry, and fishing industries has not increased as rapidly as that of the manufacturing industry, these activities provide employment for a large proportion of the population and, in addition to rendering the country self-sufficient in regard to most essential foodstuffs, are also a substantial source of foreign exchange. Corn is the most important crop in sheer size, and it is also one of the largest agricultural exports. Wheat is produced mainly in the winter-rainfall area of the Southwest Cape Province, and sugar cane occupies large areas along the coastal strip of Natal. Deciduous and citrus fruits, grown mostly in the Transvaal and Western Cape regions, are well-known South African exports; the processing of these fruits is a thriving industry. In addition, South Africa is one of the world's largest producers and exporters of wool —exports in 1963 were valued at R116 million.

South Africa (with South-West Africa) ranks fifth in the world as an exporter of fish and fish products. The fishing includes both deep-sea trawling and inshore fishing. The former is the source of hake, cod, sole, and other varieties for local consumption, while inshore fishing (an industry which has expanded enormously during recent years) consists of the catching of pilchard, mackerel, and so forth. A considerable amount of the seafood is frozen locally.

The distributive sector of the economy has expanded to keep pace with the development of industry, mining, and agriculture and the consequent growth in national spending. Influences which have made themselves felt in other advanced countries have been strongly in evidence in South Africa as well. Modern methods of marketing, such as the supermarket, have been applied with notable success; and the rapid increase in the turnover, size, and number of branches of departmental and chain stores, particularly in developing suburban shopping areas, has been an outstanding feature of the economy.

Inevitably, considerable inroads have been made into the sphere of the traditional wholesale houses. The success of local industry has lessened their importance as suppliers of imported goods, and the establishment of direct channels between manufacturer and retailer has become more common, particularly in the case of nationally marketed and advertised branded lines.

The economic achievements of South Africa since the war have largely been made possible by an exceptionally high rate of investment. This averaged 26 percent of the gross national product over the period from 1946 to 1956 and 21 percent since 1959. This investment was financed from corporate and personal savings, depreciation allowances, revenue transfers to loan account, and foreign capital. Of the total capital invested, a considerable portion has been applied toward improving and expanding essential public services such as railway transport, electric power, and communications.

As in all developing countries, the continuous expansion and diversification of the domestic market in South Africa as more and more people are drawn into the orbit of industrial and commercial activity offers the investor ample scope for venturing into the field of enterprise directed toward the satisfaction of new demands. Young, struggling South African industries are protected by customs tariffs, which are generally moderate. Government protection and encouragement has enabled numerous South African industries to become firmly established.

The present structure of the South African labor force owes its origin to the nature of the industrialization process in this country. The growing demand for labor, in the mines and in the towns and cities, has drawn large numbers of indigenous Bantu away from their subsistence environment toward the market economy. The majority of Bantu, having no industrial skills of their own, are employed as manual workers, while the trained workers and artisans are drawn from the white population. A significant portion of the Indian and Colored labor force is engaged in skilled or semiskilled industrial and commercial activities. There is, therefore, a good supply of unskilled and semiskilled labor currently available in South Africa.

South Africa has an impressive record of industrial peace. With the exception of two relatively short-lived strikes in the gold mining industry in 1946 and 1947, arising from internal dissension within the trade unions concerned, there have been no major strikes since 1922. This lack of dissatisfaction among workers is largely attributable to the advanced industrial legislation governing wages and working conditions.

The importance of raising Bantu wages in order to increase the wellbeing of the worker and to provide a more widely based market for South African goods is generally recognized in the business community, and recent investigations reveal that the real wages of Bantu employees have generally risen more than twice as fast as real wages paid to white employees for the years 1959-60 and 1960-61. The aim of industrial legislation in South Africa is to secure industrial peace, eliminate racial friction as far as possible, and secure for *all* races a rising standard of living consistent with noninflationary growth.

With regard to social welfare, there is no state medical scheme for the white population, but the majority of companies administer their own medical aid schemes. The poorer Bantu enjoys free Government medical and hospital care or, where charges are made, they are purely nominal. Baragwanath Hospital, the largest and most modern nonwhite hospital in Africa, is one of the largest specialist hospitals in the world and has more than 2,500 beds and a Bantu nursing staff of 1,200. The cost of maintaining this institution is R3.5 million per annum.

As far as other forms of social welfare are concerned, the members of the white community are eligible for old age pensions subject to a means test; if granted, these pensions are payable to males on reaching the age of 65 and to females on reaching age 60. The Government's responsibilities in respect to the Bantu, Colored, and Asian groups are chiefly connected with old age, blindness, and disability; famine relief in drought-stricken areas; and the establishment of community centers and youth clubs. Separate departments—the Department of Bantu Administration and Development, the Department of Indian Affairs, and the Department of Colored Affairs—attend to the needs and requirements of each particular group. Most employers have welfare officers to provide for the social, medical, and recreational requirements of their employees—of whatever race or color.

South Africa's plentiful coal resources enable electric power to be produced at an exceptionally low cost. About 70 percent of the power output is generated by the Electricity Supply Commission, a Government undertaking. The average price per kilowatt of its electricity varies from 1.01 cents in the Western Cape down to .431 cents in the Transvaal and Orange Free State.

In a country which has large areas of comparative aridity and very few important perennially free-flowing rivers, the securing and conservation of water supplies are naturally matters of concern. Although South Africa has some well-watered regions, the provision of water supplies adequate for the continued development of agriculture and industry usually necessitates special measures of water reticulation and conservation.

The State Department of Water Affairs is constantly working to obtain the maximum benefit from the country's water resources and has several schemes to this end under consideration. The most significant of these is the Orange River Development Project.

The construction and improvement of roads and railways in South Africa, to bridge the vast distances between the major population centers and between the interior and the coast, have been vital to industrial and commercial development. The speeding up of communications through the expansion of internal air services has also contributed substantially to economic progress. The railways are state controlled through the South African Railways and Harbors Administration, and to improve the service provided, the authorities are at present engaged in a number of electrification schemes—projects for the duplication of existing lines—and general expansion of transport facilities. South Africa has a well-developed rural road and bridge system, and the tarring and improving of roads is the constant concern of the provincial administrations.

To summarize the above discussion, while South Africa's growth in the past has been notable, the future appears to hold outstanding opportunities for even greater achievements. The country offers the foreign investor the following advantages from a strictly economic point of view:

1. Economic growth with a stable government.
2. A sound, free enterprise economy.
3. A strong currency.
4. The right of foreign investors to invest on very favorable terms, to remit current interest and dividends freely, to obtain exchange guarantees, and to repatriate capital in accordance with a flexible exchange control policy.
5. Relatively low taxation.
6. Good relations between labor and management.
7. Official policies aimed at securing economic growth with price stability.

COLGATE-PALMOLIVE OPERATIONS IN SOUTH AFRICA

The Colgate-Palmolive Company has two divisions, the domestic division and the international division. The international division, headquartered in London, has subsidiaries established in 50 different countries of the world, of which the South African company is one.

The South African company was registered in June 1929, and the sale of Palmolive Soap and Colgate Dental Cream at first took place on an indent basis. In February 1937 arrangements were made to manufacture soap under contract at East London in the Eastern Cape Province; at the same time arrangements were also completed for the manufacture of toilet articles using our own manufacturing facilities on rented premises at East London.

Because of the rapid expansion of the company, enlarged manufacturing and administrative facilities necessitated the consolidation of manufacturing operations and the office administration under one roof, and, as a result, in 1959 the present factory and office block at Boksburg was commissioned. The factory, offices, and warehouse at Boksburg cover 350,000 square feet, and the whole site consists of at least 20 acres. In addition, the company has another 51,000 square feet of leased warehousing facilities in principal cities of the Republic.

The company now manufactures and markets well-known brands of toilet soaps, detergents and washing powders, household cleansers, and a large range of toilet articles, all of which enjoy excellent consumer acceptance and sale in a highly competitive market. Scientific marketing skills are employed to introduce these products to the consumer, and a great deal of management time is given to all aspects of each product. The most attractive presentation, the most convenient package for the consumer to handle, the most effective formula, and an economical price are all elements which have to be considered by management before the product is introduced to the market. And once it has been introduced, all these aspects are continually under review to insure that the product is still living up to its original attributes and is not lacking in any of the elements important to keeping it at the top of its product class.

Colgate-Palmolive is considered one of the biggest advertisers in the Republic. There is no television in South Africa, nor is it expected to be there for at least another two years, so the advertising is in press, magazines, and radio. It has to be designed so as to appeal to each different segment of the population and cater to their particular requirements and tastes.

The sales force responsible for the distribution of our products totals 47 and comprises white, Bantu, and Asian personnel. Our coverage extends throughout the entire Republic, and each salesman reports to a district manager who is located in one of the larger towns in each sales territory. We presently employ seven district managers. These sales territories are divided into two divisions under two divisional managers, who spend the bulk of their time "out in the field" supervising sales operations. In charge of this entire sales force is the general sales manager, who is headquartered at Boksburg but who travels extensively throughout the country to keep abreast of the latest sales trends.

The bulk of our sales comes from the white market, but we are making good inroads into the great potential which exists in the large, virtually untapped Bantu market. The majority of sales to the Bantu population are conducted directly from the delivery truck or van on a cash basis, with the sale and delivery completed in one operation. Because of the lower income level, special deals and smaller sizes are designed for this segment of the community. The company's operations include a special van sales division, which comprises a European manager and a European district manager who supervise nine Bantu van salesmen. These salesmen penetrate the large Bantu complexes in the Johannesburg area and the Northern Transvaal and Natal Bantu homelands.

Government legislation prohibits house-to-house sampling and couponing in the Bantu areas. Because of this law, we have developed in-store promotions for the urban Bantu areas and rural demonstration units for the rural Bantu territories. The in-store promotion is a promotion whereby sales girls sell our products on a "Buy one, get one free" basis at high traffic stores. A hard-hitting sales story is delivered during the selling operation.

Trucks cover all major outlets in the rural areas and stage demonstration shows on our major products. To add excitement to the promotion, a dance contest is held, and then a "Buy one, get one free" promotion concludes the operation. It is not uncommon for an audience of 1,000 Bantu to attend these rural shows.

Tremendous effort is made to acquaint the Bantu with the names of our products because, in many cases, the brand name is not considered very important to them. Therefore, in all of our Bantu work great stress is laid on the names of our products to insure that, when the time comes for repurchasing, the names of our products will be firmly imprinted in their minds and that, at that time, our product will be asked for—by its *specific brand name*.

In the more sophisticated white market, promotions are conducted on a different pattern. They usually consist of single and double packs with a "price off" offer or the inclusion of an "on pack" or "in pack" coupon having a nominal value.

To keep abreast of current modern merchandising trends in the white market, we employ a crew of displaymen and merchandisers who, to encourage the sale of our products, erect massive, eye-catching displays in the larger stores and supermarkets to attract the consumer and persuade her to buy our products.

Market research studies are undertaken on a continuing basis to ascertain the extent to which our products are receiving consumer acceptance and to evaluate the positions of our products in terms of competitive product incidence and market share.

All the marketing, selling, promotional, and market research functions fall under the control of the marketing manager (who reports to the managing director) who, in addition to the previously mentioned personnel, has a well-qualified staff of marketing employees—product managers —who each handle specific products. The group product managers are divided into two sections—one section handles products for the European market and the other handles products for the Bantu, Colored, and Asiatic markets—and these two sections each have a group product manager in charge of their operations. It is the responsibility of the product managers to insure that their products maintain good sales and profit levels and good market share positions. It is also their responsibility, should there be any downward trend, to see to it that the necessary corrective action is taken to remedy the situation.

The Colgate-Palmolive plant at Boksburg is one of which we are justly proud. It is very modern and contains the most up-to-date type of machinery available for our manufacturing requirements. The bulk of the machinery has been imported from Europe, although local equipment, where available, has also been installed. In the manufacture of our products approximately 65 percent of the essential raw materials is imported from overseas, and of that 65 percent figure approximately 55 or 60 percent is imported from the United States. All our packing material requirements and the balance of our raw material needs (35 percent) are purchased from local suppliers.

The main warehouse in South Africa is situated at Boksburg alongside the plant, where we have adequate rail facilities enabling the shipping of our products to our various warehouses and depots throughout the Republic. To facilitate the speedy delivery of orders to customers, company warehouses are situated in all of the main centers; in some of the smaller towns, we find it more economical to have this warehousing and delivery operation handled by an agent.

The manufacturing operations are under the control of the manufacturing manager, a qualified chemical engineer, who has a large, experienced staff to cope with the requirements of producing high-quality products under, very often, tight production schedules. It is also necessary at times to divert swiftly from scheduled production timetables to meet the dictates of the market. The manufacturing manager is also in charge of our warehousing and distribution functions.

The financial aspects of the company are administered by the controller, who handles banking and exchange control matters, insurance, all accounting matters, and the administrative facets necessary to insure that the company is running on a profitable and sound basis. The controller holds a company secretary's diploma, and he is also a qualified cost and works accountant; furthermore several of his staff members also hold accounting diplomas.

The administrative department submits sales and profit figures to New York and London on a set date each month, and these are followed up with supporting schedules shortly thereafter. The accounting section is extremely well mechanized, and the data processing department assists tremendously by processing required statistical data necessary in the day-to-day running of our business.

The personnel manager, in addition to the hiring, control, and placement of staff, plays an important role in attending to the staff's requirements and needs. We presently have 830 employees on our payroll.

One convenience offered to the staff is a modern canteen, serving lunches each day plus refreshments during the day, which is at the disposal of all employees in each department of the company. The charge for meals is very modest; and the canteen, which is operated by an outside industrial caterer, receives a subsidy from Colgate-Palmolive each month to assist in maintaining its profitability in providing this service to the staff.

Another employee benefit is a medical aid scheme which the company administers for white employees. In line with local policy nonwhites are excluded from such schemes, as they are able to participate in free Government hospitalization and medical care. A pension plan and life insurance scheme are also operative for white employees. At the time of this writing, negotiations are being conducted to finalize the formation of a pension plan for our nonwhite employees, and this is expected to be accomplished by July of 1966.

An excellent first-aid clinic with a qualified nurse in charge is available for all members of the staff. A panel of doctors calls regularly at the clinic several times each week in case medical attention or advice is required; they are also on call at all times during the day. We are certain that the first-rate facilities which the clinic provides are instrumental in our low "sick rate" turnover.

With the exception of the managing director, who is an American citizen, and the newly appointed marketing manager, who is from Australia, the members of the management team are all local residents who received their education and training in South Africa.

It is the company's policy to expose as many of its employees as possible to outside and improved methods, and, in this regard, employees are selected to attend many of the worthwhile seminars which are organized locally. In addition to this, members of the marketing staff are selected on a biannual basis, to attend marketing courses sponsored by the international company. These are held in London, and, coincidentally with this visit, candidates spend some time in Europe studying problems and products which might have a bearing on the South African scene. With the continued expansion of our plant at Boksburg, it has also been found beneficial to send manufacturing and technical personnel to Europe to study the latest processes for possible application in South Africa.

Conversely, the South African company also assists in the training of overseas international personnel for managerial positions in related Colgate-Palmolive companies in other African states. These personnel usually come from either the United States or the United Kingdom and, after a brief training in all departments of our business, spend the balance of their training period in our Bantu marketing division to equip themselves for assignments elsewhere on the African continent at a later date. This training period lasts approximately two years, at the end of which an evaluation is made of the candidate's progress and recommendations submitted to the international company as to his potential and future career.

*   *   *

This, then, is a survey of business conditions and the scope for investment in South Africa and a quick overview of Colgate-Palmolive operations there. Some of the problems we are facing are typical of those that business in general finds both in South Africa and in Africa as a whole. It is our hope that some of these experiences may prove to be of value to other companies and managers contemplating doing business in Africa.

THE EXPERIENCE OF BRISTOL-MYERS WITH THE AFRICAN MARKET •

C. J. OMANA

IT IS DIFFICULT TO SAY when the first Bristol-Myers product was sold in the African market. We, however, have no doubt that it was Sal Hepatica, which was introduced in the United States in 1895. It was certainly followed by Bristol-Myers' forerunner in the American toiletries field, Ipana toothpaste, which was introduced 20 years later.

The methods and techniques used to introduce these products were a far cry from the marketing methodology which is employed today by Bristol-Myers in Africa and throughout the world. I am sure that the only effort that was expended was in the preparation of export documents to service orders from local merchants catering to an expatriate clientele who already knew of the product in the United States. Advertising, sales, and market research as we know these today were totally absent from the scene.

It wasn't until 1936 that Bristol-Myers commenced to "do business" in Africa. This was the year of the formation of a manufacturing subsidiary in the Union of South Africa. This subsidiary, at the outset, began marketing its products to many of the other markets of sub-Sahara Africa. The actual selling was handled by specially appointed independent distributors, and it wasn't until 1957 that a Bristol-Myers sales force was formed in South Africa.

Bristol-Myers concentrates on "specialties" rather than products which

C. J. OMANA is Manager—African-Middle Eastern Division, Bristol-Myers International Corporation, New York, New York.

fall into the "commodities" category; hence its marketing and sales efforts have been more successful among the higher income groups of the African market. The South African subsidiary reports to the African-Middle Eastern division in New York.

Today the remainder of the sub-Sahara African market is supplied from either the United Kingdom, the United States, or France. Bristol-Myers presently sells its products in these markets through exclusive distributors, who look to the company for guidance and assistance. The problems and opportunities which confront companies like Bristol-Myers in the marketing of consumer products in these areas are dealt with in the following pages.

There are 215 million Negroes living in sub-Sahara Africa, an area twice the size of the United States. In this part of Africa the whites are called Europeans, those of mixed blood are called Coloreds, the East Indians are called Asians, and the Negroes are called Africans. There are nearly 4 million Europeans, 1.75 million Coloreds, and .75 million Asians living in sub-Sahara Africa, most of these groups being concentrated in Southern and East Africa.

The African segment of the market accounts for 97 percent of sub-Sahara Africa's population. The African market itself is not homogeneous. There are over 40 countries in sub-Sahara Africa, whose peoples speak hundreds of languages. However, from a marketing standpoint there are many common denominators and some important differences.

Let's start with a thumbnail sketch of our prime target—the African consumer. The average African consumer is not sophisticated by European or American standards. There is a good chance that he cannot read or write. However, he is very quality-conscious—to the point often of even being suspicious about products. And more important, he is willing and very able to learn. This means that he is susceptible, in fact very receptive, to advertising. In other words, give the African a quality product, priced within his means, advertise it in a manner which will reach him, and you will develop a customer with an unprecedented degree of brand loyalty, as Nestlé has been able to do with its condensed milk. But in marketing to the African, one might as well throw out the book of standard practices and start from scratch. If there was ever a case for adaptability and flexibility, this is it.

For instance, regarding package design and size, the African market has its own requirements. The redesigning and changing of a successful product's package is at times highly desirable in the United States. However, it should be studiously avoided in Africa. Quite often the African has been sold inferior goods in a package very similar in appearance to an established quality product. For this reason the African looks at even the most minute deviation in package text or design with suspicion. If a manufacturer feels that he has to change his package, he should first test the new design or he may risk losing a sizable share of market.

Because the African is an excellent judge of quality, it makes good marketing sense to avoid selling him inferior merchandise. However, his purchasing power is low. The solution to this dilemma is to market low-cost, small-size units. This is precisely what we have done with our dentifrices and deodorants in Africa.

While the African can generally be described as unsophisticated, he certainly cannot be considered uncomplicated. He is subject to many influences and preoccupations which must be taken into account when one is formulating brand and company strategies.

A major preoccupation of the African is money. However, he does not want money for its own sake but rather because he believes it to be a source of power. Power is something he craves, for he has been subjugated for too long a time. In looking at the Europeans and the way they live, he has come to the conclusion that they obtained power because they have earned and saved money. I am sure that this is one of the reasons why the banks are such heavy advertisers. They are very wisely taking advantage of a tailor-made opportunity.

The African's craving for power is also behind a virtually insatiable thirst for education. He does not look to education as an end in itself but rather as a means of earning more money, which, in turn, will mean more power. If one were to pick up an issue of any of Africa's leading magazines, he would be likely to find several advertisements for correspondence schools.

Another strong influence in the African's life is his respect for things American, for America symbolizes a way and manner of life toward which he is striving. Advertisers, both local and foreign, take advantage of this fact. It is not uncommon to hear American accents and see American spelling used to advertise products.

The multiplicity of languages in Africa adds to the mounting list of variables facing the African advertiser. Because of the many languages and dialects in sub-Sahara Africa, it would obviously not be practical to advertise in all of them. However, in order to reach the markets which we are after, we have to consider advertising in the main languages, such as Hausa in West Africa; Swahili in East Africa; Susoto, Zulu, and Xhosa in South Africa; not to mention Hindi and Guarati, spoken by the East Indians, who form an important and affluent segment of the populations of East and South Africa.

UNCONVENTIONAL ADVERTISING MEDIA

It will be readily appreciated that conventional media do not reach the African so effectively or economically as they do the American consumer. This is particularly true where a new product is being introduced. For this reason, in Africa we rely much more heavily on other forms of advertising and sales promotion such as sound trucks, roving movie vans, sampling, promotional teams, and contests than we would in the United States. These are the most popular and effective media used to reach the African.

The sound truck is by far the number-one medium in sub-Sahara Africa, with the exception of South Africa where it is not permitted. These vehicles are expensive but most effective in getting the advertising story across. Some are outfitted with film projectors and offer regular movies and live entertainment in addition to advertising. This operation is not too different from the roving medicine man shows that were popular in the United States during the latter part of the last century. These vehicles also offer a springboard to other important forms of advertising and promotion, such as sampling, which is by all odds the most effective method of introducing and increasing the usage of many products.

Then there are sales promotion teams, which consist of trained propagandists stationed in special booths outside retail outlets. They demonstrate and extol the benefits of the product or promote a special offer.

And last, but not least, there are contests. This form of promotion is particularly successful with Africans, with entries running as high as 25 percent of the total readership employed. In order to be successful, contest rules should be simple, and a large number of prizes of a useful nature should be offered.

RULES IN ADVERTISING

How do we reach this market? What appeals should we use? What pitfalls must we avoid? First of all, we must adopt as basic the premise that the approach must be simple and direct. While this is a desirable principle to follow in the United States too, it is an essential one for Africa. We have to follow it much more conscientiously than we do in the United States, for what would be considered simple in America can be construed as complicated in Africa.

For instance, let us take the matter of illustrating advertisements. The first rule is to avoid abstractions, which, of course, is another way of saying, keep it simple.

A second rule is to avoid the use of perspective. Many Africans are not as familiar with perspective as other people. If shown a picture of two lions, one in the foreground and the other in the background, they perceive the illustration in only two dimensions and see only a small and a large lion. This is not too surprising when one realizes that the device of perspective wasn't mastered until the fifteenth century with the advent of the Italian Renaissance and that it was, therefore, a relatively late artistic development even in Europe.

We should also avoid the "before and after" approach. The African in his singularly logical way reasons that no one can be in two places at the same time; therefore, these two people who look a little different must be somebody and "his brother." The entire intent of the advertisement would be lost.

What about copy? Again, we should strive for simplicity. For example, we should avoid the use of alliteration. That dog food commercial that says, "It's mighty, it's meaty, it's mighty mighty meaty," would fall flat on African ears.

We should also avoid commercials which proceed at too fast a pace and which jump from one situation to another. Many Africans cannot follow them, especially those who do not possess our particular mental shorthand. That is why many American and European commercials have not succeeded with the African.

The advertiser must also keep in mind the differences in standards of values and cultural patterns. For instance, the "keeping up with the Joneses" approach would be difficult for the African to comprehend. Another difference between his culture and ours concerns the status of women. Many Africans consider that women have a much lower status than in our society; therefore, it would not be wise to appeal solely to women, for it is the man who approves of the purchase.

One would think that all this stress on simplicity and directness would take away much of the copywriter's and art director's creative satisfaction. Or does it? Perhaps in Africa the really clever creative thing to do is not to be clever.

Let's now get away from what not to do, and let's examine some of the more positive aspects of advertising in Africa. So far we have seen some examples where the African's background and habits make our selling and advertising job more difficult. There are also instances where it can help.

One case in point is in the sale and promotion of toothpaste and tooth-brushes, for Africans have appreciated white teeth and dental hygiene for a very long time. Their practice of rubbing their teeth with sticks probably goes back further than the toothbrushing habits of Europeans.

The use of totems and symbols in advertising can be very effective in Africa. The representation of animals is something which advertisers rely heavily upon in Africa, for animals symbolize important intangibles and values associated with everyday African life. Among the more popular and generally recognizable symbols among the Bantu tribes of Southern and Central Africa are the lion, the leopard, and the elephant—representations of strength and vitality. An example of a product which successfully makes use of the lion symbol is a beer called Lion Lager. During a press campaign that ran for three years in Rhodesia, the market share for this beer increased from 5 percent to 48 percent.

The African is preoccupied with health, strength, and vitality, which are commonly lumped together under the term "power." This emphasis on "power" can be equated with the widespread concern with sex appeal in U.S. advertising.

But one must realize that the African does not regard sex in the same way as the Westerner, nor is he concerned about it in the same way. Therefore, the advertiser would be wise to limit his use of the sex theme in Africa to the health, strength, and vitality approach.

We must keep in mind that the African is extremely conscious and aware of his having been exploited and fooled by unscrupulous advertisers. One of his reactions is to reject products which he feels have been specifically created for him.

It is therefore important that the advertiser convey the idea that the product being advertised is popular with the European population as well. This is fairly easy to do in parts of Africa with a large European population, for there are usually available media which reach both races, South Africa being a prime example. However, for a product to attain this essential "white man's image" in areas where the European population is negligible, such as in West Africa, will require the creation of a special atmosphere. The use of an American, European, or even a worldwide situation showing whites using the product is one way of handling the problem.

Another excellent way to convey this image is to show the product being used by Africans in ultrasophisticated European situations. The use of an African personality who has been accepted and acclaimed by the non-African world can also be employed to good advantage.

There are other solutions to the problem. A lot, of course, would depend on the product and the particular African market involved. For instance, it is possible to avoid the use of models altogether, as was recently done by one of the four successful beer companies in South Africa.

Another way is to run identical or similar ads, one showing African models and the other showing Europeans, making sure that the Africans will see both ads. One South African company accomplished this by using two billboards, one located inside an African township and the other in a "white" area on the road to the African township. The two ads left no doubt in anyone's mind that the product was for Europeans as well as Africans.

Like every other market, therefore, the African market has its special characteristics and needs. The company which understands those individual requirements and tailors both its products and its marketing strategy accordingly will find excellent opportunities awaiting in Africa.

THE CHANGING STRUCTURE OF AFRICAN ECONOMIES •

BERNARD BLANKENHEIMER

WORLDWIDE ATTENTION has focused increasingly on Africa in recent years. Names of people and places once strangely exotic, such as those of Kenya's President, Jomo Kenyatta, or the Indian Ocean "spice island" of Zanzibar, have become household words. Most Americans are aware that the political face of Africa has been drastically redrawn and that 37 independent African countries now constitute a powerful voice in world forums. Yet despite the plethora of recent literature on that continent, unfortunately for many Americans, African lands still remain clothed in an aura of mysticism, misconceptions, and misunderstandings. That this is particularly so with regard to the African economic situation largely reflects the as yet limited commercial and economic contacts between U.S. businessmen and their African counterparts. For both the U.S. business community and the United States as a whole, this is a serious matter which needs remedying.

The swift decolonialization of Africa and the resultant "power shift" from Europe to the former "Dark Continent" have created among the new African leadership an intense desire for accelerated development, which is being manifested by ambitious government capital expenditure programs and experimentation with various forms of government enterprise

BERNARD BLANKENHEIMER is Director, Africa Division, Bureau of International Commerce, U.S. Department of Commerce, Washington, D.C.

in the productive sector. Most African leaders welcome private participation in development projects, but if such assistance is not forthcoming, it is only natural that these new nations will be forced to rely increasingly on the public sector to promote economic growth. The implications of such an attachment to "statism" are only too clear.

Obviously, the U.S. business community can exercise an important role in this respect. But the benefits from U.S. involvement in Africa's economic development need by no means be one-sided. Many profitable trade and investment opportunities exist within the context of Africa's expanding economy for the entrepreneur who has the patience to search them out. And only by making such an effort now will a fair share of Africa's market be ours tomorrow. This is the challenge for American businessmen in Africa today.

BASIC ECONOMIC STRUCTURE

The African continent is second in size only to Asia and accounts for nearly 25 percent of the world's land area and about 8 percent of the world's population. The great majority of its 270 million inhabitants depend on agriculture, which has considerable potential for development. Compared with the industrial countries of Western Europe, the area of land under cultivation per person is three times as high and livestock units per capita are nearly twice as high. Other natural resources also suggest a vast potential. The continent produces nearly 14 percent of the world's mineral output, and its energy resources (coal in the south, hydropower in the center, and oil and gas in the north) are considerable.

Yet against this backdrop of wealth in land resources, the other two components of the factors of production, labor and capital, are so insufficiently developed as to make Africa one of the lowest income-producing areas in the world, with average per capita income, as estimated by United Nations sources, at about $120 per year.

Excluding the Republic of South Africa (which, though containing a little over 6 percent of the population, accounts for about 20 percent of Africa's output), the average per capita income in Africa is less than 8 percent of that of industrial countries combined as a group. And over 40 percent of Africa's income, excluding South Africa, originates in agriculture.

Historically, Africa's past economic development was largely stimulated by the needs of the former mother countries. The capital goods and skilled labor which came from the former mother country were directed toward the mines and plantations which, in turn, provided needed raw materials. Such classic colonialism, which treated Africa as a source for raw materials and a market for finished products, in effect confined economic efforts to those which furthered this objective. That is to say, roads were built and railroads constructed to bring primary export commodities to seaports, and relatively little attention was directed toward the internal needs of the African economy and intraregional or interterritorial development.

Although this is changing rapidly, one can still find different gauges of railroads, reflecting the systems introduced by the mother countries. Internal road systems often terminate at national borders with no present provision for linkages with adjacent countries. Even today, telephone communication between countries several hundred miles apart may need to be rerouted between London and Paris. And intra-African airplane routings are inadequate because the main links are north-south rather than east-west.

A further difficulty for many African economies is that not only are they dependent on the production of agricultural and mineral raw materials but often only one of these commodities is the key to the area's economic prosperity. To cite only a few examples, Ghana depends heavily on cocoa, Senegal on peanuts, Uganda on cotton, Ethiopia on coffee, and Zambia on copper. These "one crop" economies make for inherent instability because of the fluctuating price level abroad and the impact this has on financing local economic development.

Additionally, it must be noted that even within this primary production sector a large proportion of Africa's population is still directed toward subsistence activities. That is to say, although an African village may produce a cash crop for export, a good deal of the energy of its farmers is directed toward growing foodstuffs for their immediate consumption.

The underdeveloped nature of Africa and its present low income level can be construed as either a discouraging factor or a definite inducement for the U.S. trader or investor. One is reminded of the familiar story of two shoe salesmen sent to the same African country from different foreign countries. One salesman, after two days in the country, reported to his company's president saying, "There is no market here for shoes; no one wears them." The other salesman wrote back saying, "There is a tremendous market here for shoes; no one wears them."

The point here is too obvious to belabor—it all depends on your interpretation of the market condition at hand. To one, the present stage of development is but a reflection of the limitations of the market; to the other, the present stage is an indication of the potential for future development.

ECONOMIC GROWTH AND OPPORTUNITIES

Notwithstanding the relative poverty of Africa judged by present output levels, striking progress toward economic growth has been achieved. It has been estimated that in the period between 1946 and 1960 alone, external capital inflow into Africa totaled something like $15 billion, of which $9 billion represented foreign public aid and $6 billion was private capital. This spurred infrastructural development in the postwar period in ports, roads, and so forth, which is still continuing.

The process of political transition, which quickened considerably from 1960 on, ushered in new problems of nation building and has served to highlight Africa's continued reliance on external public aid, which currently is estimated to run at $1 billion to $1.5 billion annually.

Industrial gains and infrastructural improvement have drawn increasing numbers of Africans into the money economy and have led to the establishment of urban areas and an expansion of an African salaried and gainfully employed class, able and willing to purchase a wider range of consumer goods.

The interest of African leaders in economic development and industrialization is creating a market for capital goods of all kinds. Moreover, in countries where foreign exchange shortages have restricted U.S. exports in the past, the Agency for International Development (AID) program is providing an important medium through which diversified U.S. products may be introduced into new African markets.

U.S. exporters need to be aware of these trends and to take aggressive action now to merchandise their products. Obviously, market prospects for particular lines in individual countries will vary, and in some cases market penetration may need to be postponed. But the importance of "getting in on the ground floor" in Africa, where consumers have an intense loyalty, once developed, to brand names and products, cannot be overemphasized.

Africans are already consuming such highly sophisticated products as electronic computers, central air conditioning, and television. Some consumer goods take on a status symbolism; in urban areas, for example, it is rare to see an African who doesn't sport a fountain pen or a wrist watch even if he cannot write or tell time.

The important point for the U.S. manufacturer and exporter to remember is that the present low levels of consumption in Africa will inevitably be raised as the total level of economic activity expands. Consequently, the demand for an increasing array of goods and services still unknown in the African marketplace can be turned to good profit by imaginative and aggressive salesmanship.

ECONOMIC COOPERATION

It is important for the U.S. business community to understand the broad trends and countertrends current in African political and economic fields—for only thus can it adequately appraise the opportunities and pitfalls ahead. It is unfortunate but hardly surprising that there should be evidence of friction in and between states whose boundaries were determined by European colonial rivalries, whose peoples are of diverse tribes, and whose economies are weakly pivoted around agriculture. There is no question that recent political developments in a number of African states have been unsettling, but attention should not be detracted from the real progress made in economic cooperation between the newly independent states.

African leaders realize that economic development plans and projects can best succeed if wider internal regional markets can be created. Thus, despite political differences, the East African countries of Kenya, Uganda, and Tanzania have labored to preserve their internal common market and their Regional Common Services Organization, which controls all postal and telegraphic communications, railroads, and harbors. Similarly, a Customs Union has been established among the French-speaking Equatorial African states of Gabon, Chad, Central African Republic, Congo (Brazzaville), and Cameroon.

On a continentwide basis, perhaps the most important organization concerned with African economic cooperation is the United Nations Economic Commission for Africa (UNECA), which has been operating since 1958 as a regional arm of the UN Economic and Social Council. Headquartered in Addis Ababa, the UNECA has provided a forum for discussion of African social and economic problems. Its secretariat has used its expertise effectively in producing a number of valuable study papers and in organizing intra-African technical conferences and seminars.

UNECA's emphasis so far has been on the development of four sub-regional groupings—North, West, East, and Central. Detailed industrial feasibility studies are being prepared, and discussions have been held on the technical problems involved in coordinating development planning and in implementing large-scale projects, such as iron-and-steel complexes or fertilizer plants, within each subregion. At a UNECA-sponsored symposium on industrialization in Africa, held in Cairo between January 27 and Febuary 10, 1966, delegates from 25 African countries reviewed proposals for a variety of specific industries for which it was made clear private foreign capital would be eagerly welcomed in joint partnership with nations or regional groups. An African Development Bank has recently been established in Abidjan with an initial capitalization of $250 million. The bank will finance major projects of a subregional nature, in cooperation with African and foreign governments, international organizations, and private investors.

The end of the colonial period in Africa has also led to efforts to seek new relations between European powers and their former African territories in terms of broad economic—rather than political—interests. This "Eurafrica" concept has found expression through the medium of the European Economic Community (EEC).

A Convention of Association, linking 18 African countries (AOC's) with the EEC, became effective on June 1, 1964. This Convention extends arrangements originally set up in 1957, when the EEC itself was formed, by which the African territories—at that time dependencies or trust territories of the EEC member states—were able to maintain special trade and economic-assistance relationships with the EEC. The 18 AOC's are Burundi, Cameroon, Central African Republic, Congo (Brazzaville), Congo (Léopoldville), Ivory Coast, Dahomey, Gabon, Upper Volta, Malagasy Republic, Mali, Mauritania, Niger, Rwanda, Senegal, Somali Republic, Chad, and Togo.

Essentially, in the area of trade relations, the EEC-AOC Convention provides for extension of reciprocal tariff preferences and elimination of quantitative restrictions on trade between the EEC and the AOC's. An exception with regard to extension of tariff preferences to EEC products has been granted to Congo (Léopoldville) for three years, as the Congo has traditionally maintained an open door commercial policy with no preferential tariffs.

In the area of economic assistance, the Convention provides for $730 million—$620 million in grants and $110 million in loans—to be allocated to the AOC's from the EEC's Economic Development Fund over a five-year period.

TRADE IMPLICATIONS OF EEC

In Africa, the association of African states with the EEC has been received with mixed feelings. Advocates underscore the benefits African associated states will derive from it in the form of aid and a preferential market for tropical products. Critics look upon it as a privileged club from which some African states are excluded and which will involve varying degrees of market dislocation for competing producers of these tropical products.

Probably for the above reasons, certain African countries not now associated with the EEC have indicated an interest in making some form of trading arrangements with the Common Market. An important precedent in this connection may well be the negotiations just concluded between Nigeria and the EEC providing for limited reciprocal tariff preferences.[1]

To the extent that the EEC-AOC Convention provides a new source of capital and accelerates African economic development, demand for goods and services from abroad should increase in the long run; however, U.S. exports to the associated states will face an additional trade barrier in the form of a tariff preference in favor of the EEC. The U.S. concern in this respect has been noted in international forums. In general, and as put forth in the General Agreement on Tariffs and Trade (GATT) and the UN Trade and Development Board (created in 1965 as a result of the UNCTAD conference), the United States does not favor further extension of preferential arrangements and bilateral trading agreements, preferring, rather, to deal with trade and development problems facing the lesser developed countries on a worldwide, multilateral basis.

U.S. TRADE AND INVESTMENT OUTLOOK

The United States has not thus far occupied a proportionate share of the growing African market. In part this is a result of the trade barriers which in the past have obstructed and now continue to obstruct U.S. trade. Here one might cite tariff preferences in favor of the former metropole, import restrictions imposed for balance of payments reasons, and other factors rooted in the historical association with the former mother country.

Although the U.S. Government is continually seeking to reduce trade barriers, particularly those of a legislative nature, the process is slow. Equally important could be the efforts of private U.S. business to change existing trade patterns which have been institutionalized by tradition. More U.S. exporters need to visit Africa, to establish sales representatives and

---

[1] The agreement, which must yet be ratified, gives to Nigerian exports the same preferential tariff treatment in the EEC accorded the present Associated African States, except for cocoa, plywood, peanuts, and palm products, for which annual quotas will be fixed. In return, Nigeria is to give the EEC a 2 to 5 percentage point tariff preference on 26 products, including farm machinery, radios, household goods, and alcoholic beverages. Nigeria, however, is not to receive aid from the EEC.

create effective distribution channels, to provide proper servicing facilities, to introduce new products, and, in general, to excite importers about the possibilities of trade with the United States. Only by these means will the practices that have bound local business in Africa to European sources of supply be overcome.

The value of U.S. exports to Africa annually amounts to about 4 to 5 percent of our global trade. Although the relative importance of trade with Africa as a proportion of total U.S. trade has not changed significantly in recent years, the absolute value of U.S. sales in Africa has expanded rapidly. From a total of $615 million in 1960, U.S. exports to Africa had risen to over $1 billion by 1965. A breakdown by principal countries and

U.S. EXPORTS OF DOMESTIC AND FOREIGN MERCHANDISE—1965— BY PRINCIPAL COUNTRIES AND AREAS

[Value in millions of dollars. Area totals include countries not shown separately]

Africa Total[1]	1,067
North Africa, excluding U.A.R.	222
Algeria	21
Ethiopia	21
Libya	64
Morocco	55
Western and Equatorial Africa	265
Angola	13
Ghana	36
Ivory Coast	11
Liberia	39
Nigeria	74
Central and Southern Africa	580
Uganda	2
Kenya	24
Tanzania	7
Congo (Léopoldville)	70
Republic of South Africa[2]	438
Zambia, Southern Rhodesia, and Malawi	23

[1]Excludes United Arab Republic.
[2]Includes South-West Africa and British High Commission territories of Bechuanaland, Basutoland, and Swaziland.

Source: Basic Data of Bureau of Census, U.S. Department of Commerce.

TABLE 1

GENERAL U.S. IMPORTS BY PRINCIPAL COUNTRIES AND AREAS—1965

[Value in millions of dollars. Area totals include countries not shown separately]

Africa Total[1]	875
North Africa, excluding Egypt	118
Algeria	5
Ethiopia	63
Libya	31
Morocco	6
Western and Equatorial Africa	340
Angola	48
Ghana	59
Ivory Coast	46
Liberia·	51
Nigeria	59
Central and Southern Africa	402
Uganda	43
Kenya	13
Tanzania	11
Congo (Léopoldville)	38
Republic of South Africa[2]	225
Zambia, Southern Rhodesia, and Malawi	14

[1]Excludes United Arab Republic.
[2]Includes South-West Africa and British High Commission territories of Bechuanaland, Basutoland, and Swaziland.
Source: Basic Data of Bureau of Census, U.S. Department of Commerce.

TABLE 2

areas for 1965 is shown in Table 1. In absolute terms, the Republic of South Africa remains by far the largest consumer of U.S. goods in Africa, but there has been an encouraging rate of growth for U.S. exports to the newly independent and lesser developed countries, particularly in Middle Africa.

Perhaps equally significant is the increased variety of goods found in the export list. As a general group, machinery and transport equipment has constituted the most important category of U.S. exports to Africa, representing 44 percent of total exports in 1965. Food products and miscellaneous manufactured goods hold second and third place, respectively, each group accounting for 17 percent of total exports in 1965. A large part of the food exports, however, was financed under the U.S. Food for Peace program.

U.S. PRIVATE DIRECT INVESTMENT IN AFRICA BY PRINCIPAL COUNTRIES
[Millions of dollars]

Country	1960 Dollars	1960 % of Total	1962 Dollars	1962 % of Total	1963 Dollars	1963 % of Total	1964 Dollars	1964 % of Total	Percent Increase 1960-1964	Percent Increase 1963-1964
Liberia	139	15	184	14	197	14	187	11	+ 35	− 5
Libya	99	11	265	21	304	21	382	23	+286	+26
South Africa	286	31	357	28	411	29	467	29	+ 63	+14
Other countries	401	43	465	37	513	36	593	37	+ 48	+16
Percent of U.S. investment in world	3	—	3	—	4	—	4	—	—	—

Source: Office of Business Economics, U.S. Department of Commerce.

TABLE 3

U.S. PRIVATE DIRECT INVESTMENT IN AFRICA
[Millions of dollars]

Industry	1960 Dollars	1960 % of Total	1962 Dollars	1962 % of Total	1963 Dollars	1963 % of Total	1964 Dollars	1964 % of Total	% Overall Growth 1950-1964	% Growth 1963-1964
Mining and smelting	247	26	307	25	349	24	356	22	+ 44	+ 2
Petroleum	407	44	627	50	702	49	830	50	+104	+18
Manufacturing	118	13	141	11	177	12	225	14	+ 91	+27
Trade	53	6	69	6	81	6	93	6	+ 75	+15
Other	100	11	102	8	117	9	124	8	+ 24	+ 6
Total Africa	925	100	1,246	100	1,426	100	1,628	100	+ 76	+14
Total U.S. investment in world	32,778		37,226		40,686		44,343		+ 35	+ 9

Source: Office of Business Economics, U.S. Department of Commerce.

TABLE 4

Foreign trade, of course, is a two-way street, and the United States imports nearly as much from Africa as it exports to that continent—$859 million in 1965 (see Table 2). Our principal imports continue to be agricultural and mineral raw materials, including a range of ferrous and nonferrous metals and minerals and tropical commodities such as coffee, cocoa, rubber, and timber. Because such commodities are produced in many separate African countries, U.S. imports from Africa tend to be more evenly distributed among countries than our exports. For some countries, in fact, our imports exceed considerably the value of our current exports, a factor which gives added incentive to U.S. export promotion in these markets. Examples of countries in this category which have healthy trade balances with the United States are Ethiopia and Ivory Coast.

PRIVATE INVESTMENT OUTLOOK

The situation with respect to U.S. investment is similar to that with trade in that the amount currently invested in the African continent is still small in relation to the U.S. global total. However, on a percentage basis our investment has shown dramatic gains. Indeed, it is noteworthy that over the decade and a half from 1950 to 1964, the rate of growth of U.S. private direct investment in Africa has been more than twice that for U.S. private direct investment in the world as a whole. (See Tables 3 and 4.) In this period U.S. direct private investment in Africa spurted from $286 million, less than .5 percent of our global total, to $1.6 billion, nearly 4 percent of total U.S. investment abroad. In 1964, 22 percent of U.S. private investment was represented in mining activities, 50 percent in petroleum exploration development and distribution, 14 percent in manufacturing, 6 percent in trade, and 8 percent in other areas.

On the outlook for U.S. investment, it is clear that African countries are seeking to accelerate their economic development; and they realize a major obstacle is lack of either management know-how or local capital, or both. They must look to external sources for either or both of these elements. It is important for private enterprise both here and in Western countries to recognize that they can make an important contribution to African economic advancement while, at the same time, benefiting from engagement in the profitable ventures which do exist.

Private enterprise, and particularly American management, must also recognize that these newly emerging African countries tend to remain sensitive about foreign ownership's constituting a danger to their newly won sovereignty. With few exceptions, new African governments have shown themselves eager to join forces with private enterprise in partnership ventures. In the African environment, such joint public-private participation has many advantages for the foreign investor.

If such joint ventures do not take place, the danger is that African governments, impatient to develop, will become more addicted to statism as a way of achieving development. This would decrease the possibility of the emergence of an African middle or entrepreneurial class, which is so essential to the development of a democratic society.

In brief, the rapid political transition in Africa has created new market situations with challenging opportunities for participation by U.S. business to the mutual benefit of both the African countries and the U.S. commercial community. The Department of Commerce, eager to bring this message to the U.S. business community, has developed a number of promotional aids intended to help familiarize and assist American businessmen new to the African market. Publications available from the Bureau of International Commerce provide up-to-date country data, information on trade and investment opportunities, and special market studies.[2] Titles are listed semiannually in a BIC Checklist of International Business Publications available from the Bureau of International Commerce or the U.S. Department of Commerce in Washington, or from any of the 42 Department of Commerce field offices throughout the country. The field offices will also assist any individual firm needing advice or will refer them to the appropriate office in Washington.

If one can sum up advice to U.S. businessmen it would be that patience, understanding of local trading conditions, and aggressive sales techniques are essential ingredients in any successful export promotion program in a newly developing African country. The "Made in U.S.A." label is highly regarded in Africa, but it cannot be depended upon to sell the American product. Africa is now a highly competitive market.

---

[2] Among special reports in this series of general interest to U.S. traders and investors, which might be noted, are "Africa—Sales Frontier for U.S. Business," for sale by the Superintendent of Documents, U.S. Government Printing Office, at $1 per copy; and separate reports on "Market for U.S. Products in—Libya, Sudan, Liberia, Morocco, Nigeria, Ivory Coast, and East Africa," available from the Superintendent of Documents at various prices.

A JOINT VENTURE IN DEVELOPMENT •

EDMOND C. HUTCHINSON

WHY SHOULD MY COMPANY invest in Africa? What and where are the opportunities? Is the investment climate suitable? Are the basic public facilities such as roads, houses, and the like available? What assistance can be obtained from the U.S. Government? Are joint ventures a prerequisite? These and a host of additional questions face a would-be investor who contemplates spending a shareholder's money in a less-developed country.

In a brief, generalized discussion, I shall try to summarize the role that the Agency for International Development (AID) has played and seeks to play in areas of interest to foreign private investors, the interest of the United States in stimulating such investment in Africa, and some of the trends that seem to be developing in Africa which bear on investment decisions.

THE INTEREST OF THE UNITED STATES IN PRIVATE FOREIGN INVESTMENT IN AFRICA

AID periodically seeks to analyze the economies of African countries from the standpoint of projecting the needs and realistic goals of a country during the coming five years. The thrust of this effort is sensibly to direct our assistance toward gaps which are not likely to be filled by the country itself or by other "aid" lenders. It is also intended to pinpoint the steps a country can and should take to make a development program worthwhile and likely to generate results. These periodic reviews quite natural-

EDMOND C. HUTCHINSON is Assistant Administrator for Africa, Agency for International Development, Washington, D. C.

ly turn up sharply diverse findings among the African countries. However, several threads of consistency are quickly apparent. One is the relative importance of private investment as compared with "aid" investment.

For example, the importance of mineral and oil production may frequently outweigh the importance of our programs of building roads, schools, and dams and providing training in agricultural techniques or public administration. AID's input, in my view, is critical; but it is the input of the private sector that will enable some of the African countries in the not-too-distant future to finance the bulk of their own development needs. This has already occurred in Libya and is fast approaching in Nigeria. Oil and mineral production are important because of the relatively short time factor that exists between a significant discovery and the resulting foreign exchange earnings to the country concerned. Other industries, perhaps with a less dramatic short-term impact, lead to the same result. In short, AID is well aware that, while its efforts are necessary, the real development results cannot be accomplished without substantial private investment, for development is the by-product of a trained, indigenous business community.

Against this background, the interest of the United States in fostering foreign private investment in Africa is apparent. This interest is reflected by the fact that less-developed countries are to receive priority within the overseas investment guidelines.

AID'S ROLE IN ASSISTING THE PRIVATE INVESTOR

AID can help an investor in four basic ways. The first is as a source of information concerning investment opportunities. We have been aware for some time of the existence, in many parts of the world, of a large number of feasibility studies and surveys which deal with particular investment opportunities in developing countries. Some of these studies were financed by AID, but others were done by or under the auspices of international banks, foreign governments (both developed and less-developed), foundations, universities, and private firms.

AID has brought together a single listing of such studies done during the past four years and has abstracted the investment information they contain. Abstracts of more than 1,000 such studies have been prepared on report cards so that investors may easily obtain relevant information on specific investment opportunities. In some cases the cards will be available in French, Spanish, or Portuguese, as well as English, to encourage

joint ventures. The latest index was published in January 1966, and sup-
plemental sheets have been issued every few weeks.

The second tool at AID's disposal is the so-called Investment Survey
Participation Grant. The Investment Survey Program is designed to encourage American firms to explore and study opportunities in less-developed, friendly countries. If a firm does not make an investment as a result of the survey, AID pays up to 50 percent of the cost, and the survey
then becomes U.S. property. If a firm does invest, AID pays none of the
cost of the survey. Through January 31, 1966, 25 such grants have been
provided for surveys in Africa. Among the surveys approved for Africa and
resulting in a positive investment decision were those undertaken by
McGraw-Hill (Nigeria) and National Oats Company (West Africa).
Several dozen other investment surveys ranging from marine fisheries and
wood products to meat packing and metal working are under consideration.

The third form of potential AID assistance is the Guaranty Program.
Most of you are familiar with the Specific Risk Guaranty, through which
AID guarantees the investor against inconvertibility of currency, expro-
priation, and the risks of war, revolution, and insurrection. These three
guaranties are available in most of Africa's less-developed countries, and
negotiations are under way in all of the remaining countries to fill the
existing gaps. As of March 31, 1966, 179 specific risk guaranties were
outstanding covering investment in 20 African countries in an aggregate
amount of $162 million.

AID's Extended Risk Guaranty is less well known. An extended risk
guaranty can cover 75 percent of the loan capital for a given project
against credit risks as well as political risks. This guaranty is designed to
attract capital from the private money markets into investments in less-
developed countries. The extended risk guaranty can also be made available to cover up to 50 percent of an equity investment and covers the
investor against business setbacks as well as political risks. The guaranty
on equity investment has seen little use to date, and, accordingly, the
guidelines are not altogether clear. However, as a general rule, we con-
template permitting the investor at any time and for any reason to sell
his entire shareholding to AID at a price equal to 50 percent of his original
equity investment less one-half of any distributions.

The fourth tool at our disposal is well-known—that is, dollar and local
currency loans. The local currency, or Cooley loans, are available to U.S.
affiliated companies and carry maturities of up to 15 years and a rate of
interest comparable to that available at the local development banks. These
funds, which are generated from the sale of agricultural commodities, may

be used to meet a project's local currency costs and working capital requirements. Dollar loans are available to an investor that has been unable to obtain the necessary funds from either commercial sources or the Export-Import Bank. These loans, which are tied to U.S. procurement, have maturities based on the projected cash flow figures, but they normally do not exceed 15 to 20 years. The current interest rate is 5.5 percent, although the rate tends to vary according to the money market.

U.S. INVESTMENT IN AFRICA

With this rather impressive arsenal of tools in mind, we can now consider the rate of investment in Africa. By December 31, 1964, American companies had invested approximately $1.15 billion in the less-developed countries of Africa. Of this amount, approximately 75 percent went into petroleum and mining ventures. Investment in manufacturing industries was well under $300 million. While the magnitude of investment in Africa is not quantitatively small and has been increasing over the past several years at the rate of 10 percent per annum, these figures nevertheless are far from impressive when one compares them with the flow of U.S. investment into Western Europe.

There are a number of reasons for the relative lack of U.S. investment in Africa; they vary in significance from country to country. I shall mention only three. First, the investment climate tends to be poor. The reasons for this include the uncertainty of government tenure, the lack of basic public facilities, the lack of local technicians and the resulting need for large numbers of high-priced expatriates and extensive training programs, the uncertainty of judicial administration, the fear of changing tax laws and exchange practices, and the fear of devaluation. The guaranty program offsets these risks to a significant degree. However, an investor does not merely look to recoup his original investment; he looks for a long period of profitable and stable operations.

AID is and has been seeking to improve the investment climate in the African countries. It has financed basic public facilities, ranging from dams and roads to sewerage systems and electrification. We are financing programs to improve public administration and the development of integrated, reliable legal systems. We have financed schools for, and training in, basic technology, nursing, business administration, and virtually the entire spectrum from grade school to graduate school education. We are seeking to persuade African governments to establish a central point where an investor can obtain all the information and approvals required, rather than making a tour of half a dozen ministries. One could go on at considerable length about the efforts made to date and those contemplated in the future. Suffice it to say that the total spent to date by AID and all the international and national organizations is impressive in volume and is beginning to have its effect on the investment climate.

The second factor applicable to all less-developed countries in Africa, other than perhaps Nigeria and Ethiopia, is the small size of the internal market. Populations in these countries—again putting Ethiopia and Nigeria aside—range from less than 1 million to 11 million. The effective market for a given product may well be less than 10 percent of the population; thus, an export market is imperative. AID is seeking to meet this problem by coordinating with the United Nations and other institutions in the development of regional industries and little "Common Markets" in North, East, and West Africa. The effort is under way, but the path will be long and filled with setbacks. Nevertheless, the tendency toward regionalization, while in its infancy, is worthy of the investor's attention. The progress of the Central American Common Market to date and the impressive acceleration of foreign investment in those countries is a useful comparison.

I am not trying to play down the negative aspects of the investment climate or the deterrent effect of the small internal markets, but I do not believe either problem is the principal roadblock to U.S. investment in Africa. The flow of investment from Western Europe and Japan would not far outweigh U.S. investment if this were the case. Nor do I believe that the U.S. business community is less willing to accept risks or slower to recognize a good investment than are its European counterparts. Rather, I feel too few American investors—outside of the mining and petroleum industries—know of the existing opportunities. Africa remains an unknown continent to most American entrepreneurs.

AID has grappled for several years with the problem of bringing investment opportunities and investors together. The investment catalog was an outgrowth of this concern. Frankly, however, we are far from satisfied with the results of our effort to bridge the communication gap. As a result, we are looking for help from the private financial community. We are talking with leading banks and financial houses around the country and asking them to send representatives at AID's expense to African countries of their choosing for extended periods to size up the investment situation thoroughly. The thought is that these financial institutions will determine the opportunities worthy of a close look and then describe these opportunities to industrial investors for their consideration and study.

AID stands ready to assist most investors with the Investment Survey

Participation Grant Program—mentioned earlier—and to outline in general the nature of the guaranty and loan financing that would be available, given a favorable study report and financial plan. We hope to overcome the breakdown of communication at least partially by having the investor apprised of the investment possibilities by a private financial institution it knows and respects, by partially underwriting the costs of the study if an investment fails to materialize, and by providing the investor with an outline of possible financing prior to a feasibility study.

TRENDS OF INTEREST TO THE INVESTOR

One hesitates to talk of trends concerning the less-developed countries of Africa. Nevertheless, certain important developments of concern to private investors should be noted. For example, many African countries are in the process of drafting or revising investment codes for the purpose of attracting foreign investment. The rules of the game are becoming clearer. Many countries are recognizing the need for regional industries and seriously discussing the possibilities with their neighbors. The advice of the World Bank and United Nations Economic Commission for Africa concerning the critical need for private investment is being heeded. Perhaps the most encouraging indication of a change of mood is the tendency of many African governments, disillusioned by the losses incurred by government-owned and operated industries, to seek to disengage themselves from these industries and sell their stock to private businessmen, foreign and domestic. The lesson has been a hard and costly one, but in many cases the learning process has been rapid. This tendency away from government ownership and the growing recognition of the need for private investment may be the most important result to date of international and binational development efforts.

While the mood appears to be changing and the "welcome" sign is beginning to appear, the situation nevertheless requires a very high degree of industrial statesmanship. An investor should know how its contemplated investment fits into a country's development plan and consider what financially prudent steps can be taken to facilitate the country's aims. One example is the training of nationals. The tendency is for investors to train the number of individuals required to run its plant most economically, plus a contingency reserve. Often, with little added expense, the training program could be continued to provide technical know-how to be used in other sectors of the economy.

Another area for consideration, which is particularly applicable to ventures with concession agreements, is the rate of return through taxes, royalties, rents, and the like to the host country. An all-too-human tendency is to seek arrangements whereby the host country's share will be kept to a minimum. In the short run a one-sided arrangement may work well. However, the long term may be jeopardized by, in effect, inviting successor governments to seek revised arrangements. Drawing lines in this area insofar as less-developed areas are concerned is one of the challenges and fascinations of international business.

Another area calling for statesmanship is the degree of participation of the local businessmen. Not long ago the tendency was to set up a wholly owned subsidiary. More recently, investors have tended to seek out local investors to join with them. In some countries the number of individuals capable of making an investment is finite, and the question arises whether the investor should hold aside a block of stock for local investment as a business community develops or provide stock participation to its employees based on productivity. The provision of housing for local employees is another area where dividends can be reaped as a result of an effort not normally required in developed countries. All of these points and many more need consideration by an investor and bear directly on its longer-run profit projections as well as the development of the country involved.

The record of American investors to date has been by and large a statesmanlike and profitable one. We view the business community and AID as joint venturers in development. AID can and has provided considerable assistance in providing basic public facilities and training. In our view, this is a necessary foundation for the development of the private sector. However, it is for profit-minded entrepreneurs, armed with enlightened self-interest, to follow on in the development process. The result will be beneficial to the business community, the countries involved, and the broader interest of the United States in a prosperous and stable international community.

THE EXPORT-IMPORT BANK AND PRIVATE ENTERPRISE IN THE EMERGING AFRICAN NATIONS •

FOREST G. WARREN

D URING 1965, $60.8 MILLION IN CREDITS was extended to African countries by the Export-Import Bank of Washington to finance projects which will significantly benefit the economies of the countries of Africa (see Table 1). Authorizations during 1965 brought direct credits authorized for Africa since 1961 to a total of $175.2 million. In addition, long-term commercial bank credits totaling $23.1 million have been guaranteed by the Bank. These credits not only facilitate the development of Africa but also make possible exports of U.S. goods and services which might not otherwise take place. The credits encourage private investment by supplementing private funds and by financing intrastructure and service types of projects, such as power and transportation, essential to development.

The Export-Import Bank of Washington was established in 1934 by an act of Congress and, strange as it may seem in the light of international events over the following three decades, it was set up in part to facilitate trade between the United States and the Soviet Union. Political events of the time move so rapidly, however, that the Bank has never performed this original function. Today the Bank is an institution designed specifically

FOREST G. WARREN is Economist with the Export-Import Bank of Washington, Washington, D.C. This was originally delivered as a talk at an AMA Briefing Session in January 1966, and it has appeared as an article in *Africa Report* for May 1966.

EXIMBANK CREDITS FOR AFRICA—1965

Country	Amount (millions of dollars)	Project
Ethiopia	$ 4.3	Paper manufacturing plant
Ivory Coast	6.0	Aircraft for Air Afrique
Liberia	23.1	Pelletizing iron ore plant
Morocco	24.0	Phosphate mining equipment
Nigeria	3.4	Electric generator
Total	$60.8	

TABLE 1

"to aid in financing and to facilitate exports" from the United States. It is an entirely U.S. Government-owned institution empowered to perform all banking functions except that of issuing currency. It is managed by a bipartisan board of five directors who spend full time on Bank business.

The activities of the Bank are designed to facilitate the purchase of U.S. goods and services by lending dollars to foreign buyers to buy in the American market. Financial assistance is provided only after determining: (1) that the project will benefit the overall economy of the borrowing country or add to the country's foreign exchange earning ability, or both; (2) that the project is technically sound and its engineering design feasible; (3) that there is reasonable assurance of repayment; and (4) that funds are not available from commercial sources. The Bank does not make soft loans or grants, nor does it accept repayment in foreign currencies. It lends U.S. dollars repayable in U.S. dollars, on terms appropriate for the product exported according to customary commercial practice.

Since its establishment in 1934 the Bank has authorized a total of over $16 billion in direct loans. Of this total, $10 billion has been disbursed, with $1.8 billion undisbursed.

Commitments outstanding as of December 31, 1965 totaled $5.2 billion for loans and authorized credits. In addition, the Bank had insurance and guarantee liabilities of $849 million, making total Eximbank exposure approximately $6 billion.

Active direct credits, including aircraft guarantees, authorized for Africa since the establishment of the Bank total $400 million (see Table 2).

Besides authorizing direct credits, the Bank guarantees credits authorized by commercial banks and participates in the export credit insurance program of the Foreign Credit Insurance Association (FCIA). Taking these activities into consideration, the exposure in Africa of the Bank— that is, the outstanding balance of direct credits, undisbursed loans, and the Bank's contingent liability on guarantees and insurance—totals $317 million distributed in 38 different African countries or territories. This wide country coverage is due to the fact that the Bank's assistance is controlled to a large degree by the U.S. business community. The Export-Import Bank is the catalyst which helps make possible the exports which U.S. firms determine to be sound from a business viewpoint.

Most of the African countries have unusual intrinsic wealth in the form of abundant natural resources, the exploitation of which can reward not only the native state but also the foreign investor who provides the capital, plant, and equipment to develop them. Of the total direct loans and long-term guarantees of $198.3 million authorized since 1961 for Africa, nearly one-third, or $61.8 million, have been for mining and mineral-processing products as shown in Table 3.

Included in the mining and mineral-processing credits is the financing of iron-ore production in Liberia. This was an unusually large undertaking —a joint venture combining American, European, and Liberian interests. This project is now successfully coming to fruition, with promising returns to the foreign investors, and is on the verge of changing the whole economic outlook for Liberia. A second significant mining credit was for the establishment of rutile mining in Sierra Leone. As a result of this

EXIMBANK CREDITS FOR AFRICA—1934 to 1966

Country	Amount (millions of dollars)
Liberia	$ 98.3
Republic of South Africa	71.0
Ghana	65.1
Ethiopia	42.7
United Arab Republic	40.6
Morocco	24.0
Mozambique	17.0
Ivory Coast	20.3
Sierra Leone	10.2
Nigeria	5.4
Tunisia	5.0
Senegal	.3
Congo (Brazzaville)	.2
Total	$400.1

TABLE 2

AFRICA: EXPORT-IMPORT BANK DIRECT LOAN AUTHORIZATIONS
AND LONG-TERM GUARANTEES—JANUARY 1961-DECEMBER 1965

Category	Amount (millions of dollars)
Industry	$ 63.3
Mining and mineral processing	61.8
Utilities (power and water)	24.6
Hotels	3.7
Transportation (aircraft and diesel locomotives)	44.9
Total	$198.3

TABLE 3

operation the rutile industry promises to become one of the more profitable sectors of the Sierra Leone economy and a major source of income and foreign exchange.

Another major category of recent Eximbank credits for Africa is in the field of industrial development. These credits total $63.3 million since 1961 and include an alumina-processing plant for Ghana as well as textile and flour mills for Nigeria.

Reference has been made to several large projects the Bank has financed, but, in fact, no transaction is too large or too small for the Bank to handle. A large direct loan sometimes requires several months for discussions with the applicant, but a small transaction of several thousands or even hundreds of dollars may be processed under one of the Bank's various facilities in a matter of days.

A review of the Bank's programs in more detail will illustrate just how the Export-Import Bank can promote or help private foreign trade and investment. The activities of the Bank are directed toward providing three services: (1) export credit insurance, (2) commercial bank guarantees, and (3) direct credits. Let us consider each of these areas.

The export insurance program is exactly as stated—an insurance program. Exporters who ship on credit payable in not more than 180 days may obtain short-term insurance through the Foreign Credit Insurance Association (FCIA) covering their total exports. This association, in cooperation with the Export-Import Bank, insures most of the principal and interest payments against defaults by the buyer for any one of several specific reasons set forth in the policy. Eligible exporters include U.S. firms and individuals as well as foreign entities doing business in the United States.

A second type of export insurance available through FCIA is medium-term insurance covering sales on terms ranging from 181 days to five years. This insurance is generally on a sale-by-sale basis, as compared with overall coverage secured under the short-term program.

Under each of the insurance programs, the buyer usually must pay cash equal to 20 percent of the invoice value. The seller participates to the extent of a minimum of 10 percent.

The insurance programs help private investment abroad by promoting the sale of U.S. products and services abroad. They transfer to the insurer some of the risk previously absorbed by the exporter. Increasing American exports makes the foreign consumer more acquainted with American products, thus creating an atmosphere conducive to the establishment of businesses abroad using American products. Habit is a strong market factor. The establishment of a market prior to entering into manufacturing abroad is a sound step preliminary to private investment.

The commercial bank guarantee program is a program under which the Export-Import Bank guarantees repayment of principal and interest against certain specified risks on loans extended directly by commercial banks to finance export transactions. These are usually medium-term and, in some instances, long-term credits. The effect of this program on private investment is the same as that of the Bank's program for insurance. It helps in establishing markets abroad for American goods and services and improves the atmosphere for eventual private investment. However, to the extent that the credits established are to new or expanding enterprises abroad, the commercial bank guarantees have a direct relationship to promoting private enterprise abroad—a relationship described more fully in the following discussion on a third aspect of the Bank's lending program, that of direct credits.

Financing through direct credits historically constitutes the largest segment of the Bank's activity from the standpoint of the total value of assistance given. The authorized value of active direct loans and credits in Africa is $380 million, with a present outstanding balance plus undisbursed amounts totaling $271 million, compared with the Bank's liability of $46 million under its insurance and guarantee programs for Africa.

The term "direct credits" refers to loans made directly by Eximbank (or occasionally by a commercial bank under an Eximbank guarantee) whereby the lender enters into negotiation directly with the borrower. A direct loan may be for purposes of financing the dollar costs of a bridge, a large electric power station, a complex chemical plant, or a single large piece of equipment such as a dragline or a diesel locomotive. A direct loan may even be used for dollar purchases of a small plant, such as a cold storage facility, which may involve the purchase of only a few thousand dollars worth of U.S. equipment from several U.S. suppliers. These loans enable foreign buyers to pay cash to U.S. suppliers of equipment, materials, and services of U.S. origin. As stated earlier, since Eximbank's establishment in 1934 such loans have totaled nearly $16 billion and have benefited not only major suppliers but thousands of contractors and small manufacturers throughout the United States. In addition, by financing sales of products and services which would not otherwise have been exported, the Bank has made a direct, favorable contribution to our balance of payments position—for 1965 to the extent of an estimated $1.4 billion as a result of the Bank's total export credit assistance. Some $700 million of this total was from collections of principal and interest on Eximbank direct loans outstanding. An estimated additional $725 million was derived from payments made on exporter credits guaranteed or insured under Eximbank's short- and medium-term exporter programs.

The maturities of the direct loans vary from five to about twenty years, depending upon the ability of the project to generate earnings to repay borrowed capital and to some extent upon the foreign exchange position of the borrower's country. The present interest rate is 5.5 percent. This rate is subject to variation, depending on the cost of money to the Bank.

In addition to the three major programs described above, the Bank offers the following services:

1. Insures against losses from the date of the sales contract to the time that the goods are actually shipped—in other words, offers "preshipment coverage."
2. Issues guarantees on U.S. goods at trade fairs and exhibits abroad or on lease or consignment abroad.
3. Issues guarantees on the sale of U.S. technical services such as engineering studies and reports, economic surveys, and design and architectural services.
4. Extends credits to foreign financial institutions for relending to purchasers of U.S. equipment.
5. Extends emergency foreign trade loans.

The main impact of the Bank's programs on private investment is most visible as a result of the direct-loan program. The discussion of its effect on private investment cannot be divorced from the Bank's lending activity with foreign governments as the obligor. It should be stressed that the Bank does not and should not make loans—either to a government or to a private enterprise—if a private investor or a private bank is prepared to extend the credit on reasonable terms. It is possible, of course, that this principle may on some occasion have been violated, but it is not the intention of the Bank to do so in a single instance.

When is it appropriate for the U.S. Government to lend to a foreign government? This depends entirely upon the circumstances surrounding each case. In Africa one cannot overlook the political philosophies of the people of Africa and the historical origin of those philosophies. African nationalism should not be looked upon as an unfavorable trend, if in fact it is a trend. Such nationalism is nothing new. The acceptance of African nationalism is crucial in our consideration of whether or not loans to African government-owned enterprises are consistent with the Bank's policy to encourage and promote private enterprise. Traditions can be changed but should be changed only gradually. Government-sponsored enterprises such as irrigation and power projects develop resources and result in an economy more acceptable from an economic point of view for private development.

A second reason why we should not be alarmed over African nationalism from the economic viewpoint is the recognized fact that in Africa today the number of adequately trained private business people is relatively small and a large portion of those technically trained are employed by the government. The reason for this is twofold: first, the number of people who can qualify for technical training is limited and facilities for training the people are few; second, a large portion of the technically trained people are educated at the expense of the government and are obligated in many instances to serve the government. This situation leaves few trained people to organize private enterprise and, hence, in many areas the government represents the only group of technically trained individuals.

A third major factor in justifying government-to-government lending is related to the type of projects governments usually earmark for ownership —schools, roads, power facilities, transportation, and so forth. Credits for such projects directly encourage and benefit private investment. In Africa the Bank has provided financing for railway facilities and equipment in Mozambique and Tunisia; power for Nigeria, the Ivory Coast, and Liberia; and waterworks and roads for Liberia. This type of development, which is usually government-owned, is essential for the further economic development of the areas and the encouragement of private enterprise.

From these comments it may appear as though the Bank, by reason of its many loans for infrastructure development, has directly helped private enterprise very little on the African continent. What sectors are left for private investment? The major areas, of course, include mining and manufacturing. Mining is the best illustration of mixed private and government ownership and financing. The Bank always seeks maximum private invest-ment, but, once again, local conditions and national foreign policies must be taken into consideration. The Bank recently financed the purchase of $24 million worth of U.S. equipment and services for a phosphate industry in Morocco which has been owned and operated 100 percent by the Government since its establishment in 1921. On the other hand, the Bank has financed iron-ore operations in Liberia using local government capital combined with private capital from Liberia, Europe, and the United States. The size of the project was such that the Bank found that private capital was putting all the funds that could reasonably be expected into the costly venture. Eximbank's loan was necessary to make up the difference between what private capital was able to furnish and what was needed for the project involved.

When financing is provided for private ventures, the Bank makes a judg-ment on a case-by-case basis that the applicant has available a reasonable portion of the funds required for the project involved and is looking to the Bank to obtain additional dollars to supplement available funds. Using this approach, the Bank has made a $2 million loan for a textile plant in Ni-geria to supplement an equity investment by an American firm holding 70 percent of the total equity. In the Congo (Brazzaville) and in Senegal the Bank has financed two small cold storage plants in the total amount of $550,000. In these two cases the Export-Import Bank money supple-mented private American, French, and African equity. The private equity in the two plants represented 50 percent of the total equity. The Bank cur-rently has under consideration several new requests from enterprises in the private field in various African areas.

These specific cases illustrate points discussed above. In the instance of the textile mill, private equity amounted to approximately one-third of the total cost and Government equity amounted to slightly over one-tenth of the total. The sponsors of the project considered it essential to include the Government in the equity. Furthermore, the Government also con-sidered it essential to participate in order to induce private capital to come forward. What was Eximbank's role as a promoter of private investment? In this instance neither the foreign government nor the private investor was willing to invest sufficient capital to erect the size of plant which an independent feasibility study indicated was the most economic unit to con-struct. The Bank's loan constituted a catalyst for the private investment.

In the second illustration of two small cold storage facilities, the Bank's loans again performed the function of a catalyst by helping private invest-ors with numerous small facilities to establish two new plants which would otherwise not have been established. No government equity was involved.

These specific cases illustrate the areas in which the Bank has been and will continue to be useful in helping private investment. However, in each case the Bank's basic criteria were adhered to:

1. The loan offered reasonable assurance of repayment.
2. The capitalization structure of the applicant was sound from the lender's standpoint.
3. The enterprise was of economic and productive value to the country involved.
4. The proceeds of the Bank's loan were used for the purchase of U.S. goods and services.
5. Funds were not otherwise available.

THE PROBLEM OF AFRICANIZATION •

TORE ROSE

THE TOPIC OF MANAGERIAL AFRICANIZATION is a broad one and cannot
be done justice in a few pages, particularly when written under the con-
straint of not being able to undertake field work. This paper therefore
focuses on a few specific issues which seem to be of particular relevance.
Most of the ideas presented here are the result of interviews and correspondence with people who have had extensive firsthand experience
with private enterprise in Africa, most of whom the author was able to
talk to in New York and Boston. It is therefore hoped that the result is of
practical relevance. However, the writer's bias is apparent in many places,
and for this he takes sole responsibility.

It should be emphasized that the following is concerned only with the
independent countries of tropical Africa, and most of the material relates
primarily to the countries previously under British rule.

1. WHY AFRICANIZE?

"The chances of survival for Western firms in Black Africa will be determined largely by their tempo of Africanization."—Professor, Lovanium
University, Leopoldville.

"The really basic argument is this: it's cheaper."—AID Official.

TORE ROSE originally prepared this chapter as a report in fulfillment of the requirements for a master's degree in business administration, Graduate School of Business
Administration, Harvard University, under the direction of George C. Lodge, Mr.
Rose has accepted a position with an American pharmaceutical firm in East Africa
and will take up his duties in the fall of 1966.

First of all, what is meant by Africanization? For our purposes it is the replacement of whites, whether American, European, or African-born (the group will be generically referred to as expatriates, although this is an oversimplification), by Africans in middle and top management positions in privately owned companies, with the emphasis here on American companies which have their headquarters in the United States. We say "middle and top management" in order to focus on those people who, by decisions based on formal authority, can affect the deployment and profitability of a significant portion of a company's assets.

The term "Africanization" in this sense has been used for very definite reasons. It will become apparent that a very significant reason for the drive to Africanization is the question of the *power* that individuals have to influence the economic, political, and social life of a country. Anyone who commands economic resources has power over others through the manner in which he administers those resources, particularly in Africa where the total of active resources is comparatively small. There are those who are very aware of the implications for their country that the wielding of economic power has had in the past (perhaps exaggeratedly) and may have in the future. These people are the African politicians and administrators who have risen to influential positions after independence, and their *raison d'être* for Africanization is that such economic power shall be wielded by Africans and, more particularly, Africans who are nationals of their country. It is therefore essential to view the question of industrial Africanization in terms of those managerial functions invested with power.

There is a second reason for choosing the term "Africanization." The process described in our opening paragraph is sometimes referred to as "localization" or "nationalization," particularly by international bodies such as ILO. In global terms, these expressions are undoubtedly most apt, and they also gloss over the more unpalatable aspect involved: the color of a man's skin. But man is not entirely rational and open-minded, and to suppress the color aspect is a disservice to a frank discussion of the problem. It is, after all, rational to take account of irrationality, and "Africanization" is a more honest characterization of the process being considered here.

It should further be pointed out at this stage that it is not only a question of the classically "white" and their positions in business enterprises. There are also very significant numbers of other non-Africans (in the sense in which we use the term) on the commercial scene. In West Africa, these are mainly Levantines and Mediterraneans, and in East Africa they are of Asiatic origin, mainly Indian, and these groups do cause some of the same frictions that whites do. It must be remembered too that "Africa" and "the Africans" are simply names for a vast land mass and its peoples, who can be as different as Turks and Irishmen.

The company viewpoint. The incentives for a company to Africanize fall into four main categories: cost, environmental problems, expatriate personnel problems, and public relations.

The clearest and apparently strongest incentive is that of cost. Americans working in Africa expect, and get, the same salary for their work as they would in the United States, plus additional remuneration in the form of a straight allowance or generous fringe benefits. The most common procedure for determining the salary level of a national is to make use of community surveys which establish a range for persons with a given background and experience and then to offer a salary in this range (generally a little above the civil service rate). The result will be 35 to 60 percent of the U.S. rate, and it is evident that American companies are reluctant to offer compensation much above the "appropriate range." Many go to greater trouble, and incur greater costs, in training Africans for management positions than would be the case with American trainees; however, the general opinion is that the net savings are still very great.

The most pressing environmental impetus to Africanization is the power of governments to limit the number of expatriates that may be employed. Almost all independent African countries have laws (for example, the Nigerian Immigration Act of 1963) whereby the authorities may limit the employment of nonnationals in private business in terms of a percentage of total personnel or payroll, and sometimes there is the limitation that the foreigner must have an advanced degree. There may also be laws which require *new* foreign companies specifically to train and promote African employees (as is the case, also, in Nigeria).

A more general environmental reason for Africanization is simply the idea that nationals are in a better position to understand and deal with government, unions, customers, and the like. (The danger of an extremely reactionary national, who causes more trouble than the expatriate, is not present in Africa in the way it can be in Latin America; Africa does not have the same class-oriented traditional economic aristocracy.) The argument seems reasonable *a priori* and appears generally true. In one respect, however, there may be a big drawback: Nationals are "stuck" in the country; usually their families, assets, and futures are there. As a result, they are much more susceptible to pressures from local groups than are expatriates. And the government can put the screws on a national more threateningly; an expatriate can always get out. Furthermore, where there is a fairly rigid social structure, an expatriate may be able to operate out-side it, while a national must work within the constraints it imposes. It is notable that one large European processed-food company feels that its own expatriates are better able to handle the environment than are the nation-als.

A company may have an incentive to Africanize simply because of a shortage of high-quality Americans who are willing to abandon opportuni-ties at home for the relative obscurity of another continent. To leave the head office is to leave the seat of power and influence, and for the ambitious and capable man this may be too high a price to pay in terms of promo-tion prospects. So the kind of man who *is* willing to work overseas is the second-stringer, who is attracted by the special benefits which become more attractive because he has little prospect of gaining them through promo-tion at home. He is just "interested" in Africa and wants the adventure and the opportunity to get rich. In the period after World War II there has certainly been a decrease in this caricatured expatriate, but in trying to guard against the problem it is clearly advantageous for a company to employ nationals.

Finally, in view of the local pressures to Africanize, it is clearly good public relations to do so. A "good citizen" image will be fostered by being in the vanguard of Africanization; in fact, the quotation at the head of this section may indicate that more than a good image is at stake. The tempta-tion in pursuing an image is to make political promotions, to put Africans in conspicuous and supposedly managerial positions while in fact depriving them of any real influence and authority (although the Nigerian manager of a shoe factory—40 percent U.S.-owned—claims that money and title are more important than de facto responsibility; one gets the feeling that outsiders are sometimes more concerned over political promotions than the men involved). More creatively, it is often found that the public rela-tions manager is one of the first posts to be Africanized.

There are, of course, a number of reasons against Africanization from the company's point of view. The main argument revolves around the question of loyalty to the company and the possible character weaknesses of human beings. (But, when a U.S. oil company found itself nationalized in Syria, the Syrian manager resigned rather than serve in the public corporation.) Another argument is that the home office can better deal with Americans since they talk the same business language and may know each other from working together in the United States. To Africanize would mean confusion and inefficiency from the communications stand-point. The solution to this problem would also overcome another objection—that the nationals do not have enough experience; that is, they have not been exposed to the whole operation, particularly at the American end. An increasing number of companies are sending Africans to the United States for working experience, and this should have a big payoff. All the same, some deterioration in efficiency must be expected when undergoing an Africanization program.

These objections are clearly related to the question of control, which is of great concern to the company. The last expatriate bastion to fall has nearly always been the position of controller—except for the most senior managerial position, which has not yet fallen at all. The worry is that expense accounts will run riot, brothers-in-law will draw fat salaries for nonexistent jobs, and so on. But such worries do seem overexaggerated: the time when Africans might be in a position to get away with such things is still so far in the future that if, by then the company has not developed men it can trust, it has only itself to blame.

The African viewpoint. "It is the natural ambition of African governments to Africanize the principal cadres of three main sectors—the civil service, the professions, and industry. Of these, the civil service has the highest priority, and the professions the lowest."[1] In terms of power, this ordering of priorities is clear. The civil service is the agent that will implement the political decisions of the party in power, and once independence is gained, political power has been "Africanized." The stumbling block to the exercise of this power is the civil service; therefore, this is the next to be Africanized. The business sector can be influenced by political decisions, but because it wields power in its day-to-day administration of economic resources, it is thought that such power ought to reside in the hands of nationals. Finally, engineers and doctors supply a scarce resource which is not invested with a great deal of power, and they are usually welcomed or at least tolerated.

The Africanization of the civil service has uniformly been of first priority, and in many recently independent countries it has been carried quite far, although some feel there is still a long way to go. But certainly the principle has been established; the problem is now more the technical one of finding suitable Africans.

Today the pressure for Africanization is increasingly turning toward the second source of external power over internal affairs: private foreign companies. "It is sad but evident that for the cohesion of a unit, whether nation, race or continent, the invention of a common threat is neces-

[1] Hunter, Guy, *The New Societies of Tropical Africa,* Praeger, 1962, p. 247.

sary. . . . The newest nations in the world are in Africa, and the common threat they recognize is neo-colonialism . . . white domination through economic or clandestine political means . . . the repeated slogans of Africanization, non-alignment and positive neutrality may be the direct consequence of this fear."[2] The U.S. Embassy in Nairobi reports that "Africanization . . . describes *the most important* aspect of the present economic change in Kenya . . . the transfer of land, jobs, positions and status formerly held by Europeans and Asians to Africans [emphasis added]."[3]

It does not appear that any American company operating in Africa troubled itself to think seriously about an Africanization program until about three years ago, and many are only now becoming aware of the problem. But the pressure for managerial Africanization is on, and it will become greater as more Africans can claim that they are qualified to become managers on the basis of their education. There is no reason to believe that a country's leaders will not consider the Africanization of management, in due course, to be just as important as the Africanization of the civil service. Unlike the situation in the civil service, the principle of managerial Africanization is not yet established; until this is done, political necessity may force governments to take an increasingly strong stand in the years ahead.

Unless the presently mixed economies of Africa were to move toward complete state control—and recent events indicate not—foreign enterprise will constitute a significant economic sector for years to come. Politically, this is a delicate situation, as can be seen in Canada and more recently in France. And is there any reason to treat the national sensibilities of the emerging African nations more lightly? If anything, their more precarious sense of nationhood needs to be accorded more respect than Canada's or France's. Certainly a Machiavellian can see that he need not do so in terms of power politics, but it is doubtful if that would be in his long-term interest. Realistic African political leaders have shown their awareness of the benefits that foreign capital can bring; it is up to foreign companies to reciprocate the realism and offer a *quid pro quo* for being allowed to continue presumably profitable operations: they must actively pursue a policy of Africanization. We have referred to Africanization in terms of power; in the case of business this means those who visibly wield power. With good men, ultimate control can still be made to reside in the United States as has control of American operations in Europe.

[2] *Daedalus,* Spring 1966, pp. 678-679.
[3] U.S. Department of Labor, Bureau of Labor Statistics, *Labor Developments Abroad,* January-February 1965, p. 18.

2. SUPPLY AND DEMAND

"It is said that there is only one Tanzanian over the age of 42 with a university degree—his name is Julius K. Nyerere."—Report on Management Training in Africa.

"We know that in a few years we will be in deep trouble over a lack of Africanization, but there is simply nothing we can do about it."—Executive of U.S. Company with a $55-Million Investment in Africa.

One all-pervasive problem runs through the social fabric of African nations: education.

Tanzania estimates a net output of six graduates in commerce and business administration annually for the next five years.[4] For accountancy graduates the figure is 11; for economics graduates, 20; and for engineers, 34. Of these, only the engineers (8 out of 34) will include graduates from the University of East Africa's Dar-es-Salaam campus, the only university in Tanzania; all the others will graduate from foreign institutions. In 1962 Malawi did not have many more than 30 graduates,[5] and, at independence, Zambia had 100. Zambia estimates that there will be a total of only 400 to 500 graduates in 1970, in *all* disciplines, against a need for about 5,000.[6]

East and Central Africa are worse off educationally than West Africa, where Ghana stands as the most educationally developed of all African nations, with thousands of graduates. Nigeria is probably the country where most American interest has been shown, and it had an estimated 722 university students in 1957 (these being the ones who might now be at a middle management level) and 3,503 in 1963.[7] Technical and vocational students numbered 5,610 in 1957 and 31,870 in 1963.

It is therefore evident that in absolute terms the number of Africans with advanced education is appallingly low for countries of such size (Tanzania has a population of about 10 million, Malawi and Zambia 3.5

[4] Directorate of Development and Planning, Office of the President, United Republic of Tanzania: "Survey of the High-Level Manpower Requirements and Resources for the Five-Year Development Plan 1964-65 to 1968-69." Unpublished, 1964.
[5] Hunter, *op. cit.*, p. 245.
[6] These and later figures for Zambia are drawn from: (1) Zambia Ministry of Education, *Annual Report,* 1964; (2) *Transitional Development Plan for Zambia,* 1965; (3) Zambian *Digest of Statistics,* 1965; (4) "Manpower Survey of Present Occupations Requiring Form II and Above," unpublished.
[7] Adapted from Diejomoah, Victor P., *Economic Development in Nigeria,* Princeton, 1965.

million each, Ghana 7 millon, and Nigeria 55 million). Exact comparisons are difficult to draw from the available data, since some sources give figures on *rate* of graduate turnout, others on *total* number of graduates, and still others on the number of students for an advanced degree at any moment of time, which must be divided by 3 or 4 to get a turnout rate. Furthermore, it is often not made explicit whether the figures include all students in foreign countries or only domestic students. For example, one suspects that the figure for Nigeria does not include all students abroad, since statistics normally only include those on scholarships.

Before moving to the demand side, a further comment must be made in respect to the supply of Africans with advanced training. The point is frequently raised that the problem is not so much a shortage of university facilities but a shortage of secondary school education. With this bottleneck, little will be accomplished by expanding facilities for advanced education or giving scholarships for study abroad. "It is useless to offer more university places to countries where every student who can reach the necessary standard is already assured of a place, and this is roughly true [as of 1962] of the whole of East and Central Africa and Northern Nigeria."[8] For example, the Zambian picture looked like this if we take a time slice of the year 1964:[9] Seventy percent of the population entered primary school, 21 percent of these finished, 11 percent of those completing primary school started secondary school, of which 2 percent passed their "O" Level examinations (a qualification somewhere between junior high school and a high school diploma in the United States). Thus, of the *total* population, only 0.032 percent got their "O" Levels, while 33 percent *could* have entered a secondary school, which leads to this qualification, if opportunity and motivation had been present. From 1966 on, "O" Level will lead directly to admission to the new University of Zambia, which will include degrees in business, public, and social administration in its curriculum.

Opposing viewpoints. The demand for African managers can be approached from two different viewpoints: (1) the number of African managers that companies express a desire to have and (2) the number of African managers that the Africans would like to see. The former is difficult to pin down; there are differences between the expressed wishes of, and the action taken by, expatriate firms. The latter measure simply boils down to a wish for complete Africanization, and the extent to which

[8] Hunter, *op. cit.,* p. 253.
[9] See Note 6.

these firms are falling short in this respect is therefore measured in terms of the number of expatriates in managerial jobs. Clearly, complete and immediate Africanization is not thought feasible; this is a long-term goal.

It is true that companies always express a desire to employ more nationals. However, they say that it is not possible to find people who are suitably qualified. Irrespective of the qualitative factors involved, this must reflect a significant quantitative shortage. But there may also be a more directly pressing demand: the need to fill places where the authorities have refused entry visas for expatriates and the company *has* to find nationals. Even under such conditions, a job may remain unfilled. The authorities then say: "Train someone." In this way, the pressure is kept up, and the company is also forced to help the government in its educational program. It is nearly impossible to bring, say, secretaries into Nigeria now, and such pressure can be expected to creep up the organizational ladder. The groundwork has been laid in that the policy of most countries requires that "if there is an African who can do the job, he must be hired." So far, realism regarding qualifications has tempered the imposition of such pressure at higher levels.

Viewing the problem in terms of the eventual replacement of *all* expatriates, we have, for example, the following figures for Zambia:[10]

Category	1964 Stock	No. of Africans Included	1975 Requirement
Personnel officers	373	70	528
Professional accountants	435	2	984
Commercial administrators and executives	695	39	1,987

Nigeria shows a higher percentage of nationals:[11]

Category	Expatriate (1963)	Nigerian
Accountants and auditors	386	509
Senior managerial and administrative (private)[12]	2,116	1,590

Reliable and comparable figures are difficult to obtain, but even so, the

[10] See Note 6.
[11] Proehl, P. O., *Foreign Enterprise in Nigeria,* University of North Carolina Press, 1965, p. 99.
[12] International Labor Organization: *Survey of Management Training Needs and Facilities in Some African Countries 1964,* Management Development Series No. 4, Management Development Branch, Human Resources Department, Geneva, 1965.

message stands out clearly: with a country's desire to Africanize, demand far outstrips supply.

Numerically, the problem of Africanization is a big fish in a small pond, but not so big in absolute terms. There is also this facet to the problem: Although the percentage of African managers will increase, the number of expatriates may not actually fall for some years yet, since the expanding business sectors will need an increasing number of managers. Caught in the opposing trends of growth and Africanization, Nigeria expects the peak number of expatriates to occur around 1970.[13] On the other hand, Tanzania much more optimistically forecasts a 2 percent per annum absolute decline in expatriates in the private sector, with complete self-sufficiency in all high-level manpower by 1980.[14] Granted that foreign companies have some say in the matter, this certainly looks unrealistic since official thinking assumes that B.A. graduates in the humanities and arts will supply 65 percent of this high-level manpower in industry on the basis of an equal division between government and industry. Only the other 35 percent will have degrees in commerce, business administration, accountancy, or economics.

This points up a critical problem area which can lead to mutual suspicion: What the government considers a qualification to be a manager will, as in the case of the B.A. just cited, not mesh with what the expatriate considers a qualification. Maliciousness is not involved; it is simply that the authorities may not be fully aware of the real requirements of business.

What can foreign companies do? Here is an issue where foreign companies can take a stand in advance. First, they can make themselves thoroughly familiar with all the existing special programs, outside the regular educational system, which are related to their needs for trained Africans. These are numerous, and only a few are mentioned here.

In the international sphere, ILO and the UN Special Fund have been active in the area of management training.[15] They are beginning consultancy and advisory services which are very valuable in spreading good management techniques. Clearly, expatriate companies can both offer their help in these programs and be alert to Africans who have received training. Under a UN Special Fund program in Uganda, the Government of Uganda will establish a governing board on which *any private organization* which can contribute to its success may be included. Such openings

13 *Ibid.*
14 See Note 4.
15 See Note 12; also, Management Development Series No. 3, *The Effectiveness of ILO Management Development and Productivity Projects.*

should not be missed by foreign companies which are concerned with developing African managers; they provide an excellent opportunity to enter into a cooperative dialogue with governments and universities.

The complaint is sometimes heard that business routines, rather than administrative and decision-making skills, are taught in the developing countries. By active participation in these programs, however, businessmen can make their influence felt regarding the type of education they would like to see. Furthermore, foreign companies can make their own position more secure by working through the proper organizations to strengthen ancillary industries. In this way, the foreign companies will become more important in the continuing prosperity of their whole economic sector, and the government will have a greater interest in maintaining the companies' stability.

English-speaking territories have seen both the greatest pressures for, and advancement of, African managers, especially in the larger expatriate companies. It is precisely these companies which have been in the vanguard of management development. Extensive internal programs are probably not within the range of most U.S. companies, which are as yet not large enough to sustain them. But at Ibadan in Nigeria IBM has made a notable effort at management education jointly with the University. Here IBM has financed, built, and staffed a program under which about 50 men from English-speaking African countries take an 18-month course in EDP and related academic subjects. The program is considered equivalent to a three-year university course, which is normal for a bachelor's degree under the British system. All students are on full scholarship after having been selected at a 1 percent acceptance rate, and they have no commitment to IBM at the end of the course—in fact out of the first class, fewer than ten subsequently joined IBM. It is intended that after a few years the facilities will be turned over to the university free of charge.

The large oil companies also report considerable financial contributions to training programs that are not wholly internal, as well as donations to universities for technical and business education. As an example of a joint undertaking, a cooperative bank management training program has been set up in Nigeria by eleven banks and the New York University-supported Department of Business Administration at Lagos University.

There is a strong argument for bringing potential senior African managers to the United States, not only to teach them techniques but, more importantly, to expose them to a fully developed industrial system at work; "broadening the whole mental horizon for men who have seen too little of the context and atmosphere of the institutions of industry and commerce

into which they have lately moved."[16] Many companies report programs
of bringing Africans to the United States, either to train them within the
company or to have them study in academic institutions, often without
obligation to the company upon completion of the training. On a more
coordinated basis, the Council for International Progress in Management
has a program to train graduates from developing countries for one year
in American industry, with the condition that employers pledge not to
hire them afterward. For younger trainees this can be very beneficial in
instilling the attitude that one is judged by what one produces, rather than
by who one is socially—an attitude unfortunately easy to absorb from
certain cultures. It would, of course, be a good short cut to recruit directly
among African students who are in the United States of their own volition.
Surprisingly, many companies are only now waking up to this possibility.
It is also notable that one company operating in West Africa has had quite
satisfactory results by recruiting among returning students who have failed
to get their degrees abroad.

There are two cases of Africanization which illustrate a different
approach from the power-based concept which is the theme of this paper.
One of them involves Firestone, a company which has come under some
criticism for its policy of providing only low-level training in Liberia. The
other case is that of FRIA in Guinea. This concern spent some half a
million dollars on training nationals over the period 1960-1963, yet this
was at a maximum in terms of supervisory positions. In discussing the
program, Allan Hovey[17] writes: "Africanization . . . is the byword and core
of a second phase in Africa's independence movement." If the implementa-
tion reflects what is believed to be meaningful "Africanization," a communications problem exists with those Africans who agitate for Africanization.

As for more novel suggestions of what foreign companies can do, the
idea has been put forward that it should be made the normal duty of
expatriate managers to specifically train Africans to take over their posts.[18]
This would involve teaching each expatriate how to teach his understudy,
freeing the expatriate from other duties to have time to instruct the African
and giving the expatriate guarantees about his future once the African

[16] Hunter, *op. cit.*, p. 262.
[17] Hovey, Allan, "Industrial Africanization: A Case Report," *Africa Report*,
December 1963.
[18] Vuerings, Raymond, "Problems of Industrial Management in Developing Countries," *Management International*, No. 4, 1964.

steps in. In setting up new operations, where there is more flexibility, this would mean setting up two parallel lines of management, one African and one expatriate. Strangely enough, the one place where a course is to be found in this technique is on the Ivory Coast, where Africanization is a relatively dormant issue. This is the Centre de Formation et de Perfectionnement du Personnel d'Encadrement, in Abidjan.

Another source of managerial manpower is the small independent African businessman. Governments are already looking to this group as a source of replacements for expatriates. The business can often be handed over to a brother, a cousin, or even a wife. Foreign companies should be aware of this source of talent—which may be forced on them by impatient governments—and, by their contribution to the advisory and educative services mentioned, they can help to develop it.

In concluding this section on what expatriate management can do to overcome the shortage of nationals, let us quote a student of American business in South America: "Success in developing nationals depends far more on the willingness and effort of overseas executives than upon any formal home office programs or sophisticated techniques. They will be more successful in this crucial responsibility if they *must* develop nationals, and they will be especially successful if positive personal incentives are provided by their home offices."[19]

3. THE DYNAMICS OF AFRICANIZATION

"I don't know of a single instance where an African is the top man in control of expatriate capital."—Expatriate Personnel Manager of a Large U.S.-based Company

"We have a definite policy of Africanization."—Answer Given by Every Company Questioned

Hunter estimates that in West Africa 15 to 20 percent of the managerial level has been Africanized, with a lower figure for East Africa, giving a rough overall estimate of 10 percent.[20] This, however, includes publicly owned enterprises, where Africanization may be expected to have proceeded more quickly. Perhaps an overall figure of 7 percent and a West African figure of 11 percent are rough equivalents for the private sector.

Very obviously, the Africanization process has not reached any great

[19] Shearer, John C., "Overseas American Managers—Necessities or Luxuries?" *Princeton University Conference, Industrial Relations Section,* Nov. 23-24, 1959.
[20] Hunter, *op. cit.,* pp. 190, 226.

dimensions. But, though it may be a small issue now, it will grow very rapidly in the coming years. When the pressure was on to Africanize Kenya's civil service, the number of Africans rose from 3.6 percent in 1960 to 30 percent in 1964.[21]

Once more we come up against the problem of defining "management" here, and unfortunately very little can be done other than to obtain job descriptions for every man making up the statistical framework. For the present, "management" will have to be accepted in whatever sense the company involved uses it; this will probably slightly overstate the number of Africans in positions invested with significant power.

The large European companies in English-speaking Africa are often pointed to as being highly Africanized. As an example, 7 percent of the management of Shell in Nigeria was Africanized in 1957; in 1965, the figure was 55 percent.[22] On the other hand, two large internationally owned raw material concerns, one with more than 20,000 African employees, have only one African manager each. One of these reports making efforts to recruit Africans from U.S. universities, but so far only one of the recruits has reached the first step of the management ladder. And a large U.S. oil company reports that 2 out of 20 managers in Nigeria are Nigerians, but that they do not have any African managers at all in other countries.

Perhaps significantly, an American company which has relatively sophisticated products and is a relative newcomer to Africa reports 36 percent Africanization, with 59 percent of the Africans being university graduates. The personnel manager has had experience in civil service Africanization and has been concerned to promote it in the company. But another company with extremely sophisticated products reports only three Africans in a management group of 172 (1.7 percent), although one of these men is the senior manager in one of the African countries in which the company operates (responsible, however, to an expatriate superior within Africa).

Interestingly, many companies point to one or two Africans on their local boards of directors. In one case the man involved is also a manager, but usually he is a prominent local figure such as a respected lawyer or a city mayor. It is doubtful whether these men exercise much power in the company; more likely they exist to provide informal contact with local groups.

[21] See Note 3.
[22] Geiger, T., and Armstrong, Winifred, *The Development of African Private Enterprise,* National Planning Association, Pamphlet 20, 1964, p. 75.

From such a limited sample, no conclusions can really be drawn other than to report that the attitude of the company is a critical variable. It should be pointed out, of course, that it is important to consider exactly where on the management ladder the Africans are. Their density is increasingly rare in the upper echelons. Nigeria and Ghana probably have the highest-placed Africans, but no instance is known where an African holds the senior position in managing foreign capital.

Attractiveness of civil service. It is a commonplace among those conversant with the question of Africanization that not only was the civil service the first sector to be Africanized but it still has the most drawing power for the educated élite. The most talented Africans will first turn to the civil service as a career—to the detriment of the needs of the private sector. One of the low-Africanization companies just mentioned tells of an instance where it had been negotiating to bring three older Africans straight in at a middle management level, only to have the men join the civil service.

What accounts for the attractiveness of the civil service? Primarily it is a question of status—particularly, higher status at an earlier age. In many cases, external pressures also contribute heavily, both formally and informally. For example, a student returning from overseas may be obliged to give the government first call on his talents.

The fewer well-educated Africans there are and the more newly independent the country is, the more this problem increases. With fewer members of the educated élite, the road to the top is quick in an Africanized civil service, with all the attendant privileges and opportunities to exercise influence. The government of the country is the focus of power and represents national sovereignty incarnate. Families, friends, schools, and the government itself will often foster an image whereby management in private companies does not even seem to be a feasible alternative. The system of family obligations in most African countries is such that families with a well-placed connection in the civil service may reasonably expect to benefit and naturally will press their sons into such a career. The additional factor of resentment and suspicion against foreign capital, most pronounced in early independence days, adds to the unattractiveness of a career in the private sector. Moreover, there may simply be uncertainty in an African's mind that the foreign firm will continue to operate: the public sector offers much more security than American companies in particular, where firing is much more common than in European companies. Finally, since Africanization first takes place in the civil service, higher positions may be expected more quickly than in a foreign company top-heavy with expatriates who show little sign of moving. At least one can be sure that the civil service is expanding, while an established company may have static personnel requirements.

This picture is undergoing some change now, particularly as civil service posts are being filled with youthful Africans; as a result, quick promotion begins to look less likely to a new entrant who is faced with many layers of superiors not much older than he. Also, as the country settles down after independence, foreign capital may become more appreciated as being beneficial to the domestic economy. But these factors, especially the former, inevitably mean greater pressure for Africanization as the educated, impatient for positions of influence, see an influential sector still dominated by foreigners.

A distinction is sometimes drawn between the Africanization of the civil service and of private business in terms of the problem of efficiency. As a result of replacing expatriates with insufficiently trained Africans, efficiency is bound to drop, and the argument runs that while the civil service could tolerate this, a profit-oriented private business cannot. On the other hand, it is also argued that the whole pace of business life is slow in Africa and, therefore, personal efficiency is not so important as in the United States. In any case, a temporary loss of efficiency should be measured against the permanently lower cost of African managers.

Progress up the ladder. The position of personnel manager is the one most likely to be Africanized first, the view being that in this position an African is best able to deal with problems of recruitment and human relations; that is, problems of racialism, tribalism, community organization, and family loyalties. This is often true, but there have been cases where an African accepting this job is regarded by fellow employees as a traitor to his tribe or community and loses their confidence. Only expertise, based on sound training, can alleviate such a situation, and this expertise is found mostly among those who have been trained abroad, though domestic training schemes are increasingly evident—such as the Personnel Management Advisory Service of the Federal Ministry of Labor in Nigeria. Outside the personnel function, office staffs and commercial posts are most quickly Africanized; it is especially noticeable that West Africans have a penchant for trading activities. Regrettably, it may also be that these organizational posts carry fewer problems than others, since African economies are characteristically a seller's market. In areas such as finance, control, production, and industrial engineering, Africanization is much slower and training facilities are fewer.

The size of the company is a relevant factor; the very largest are able to set up internal training schemes, the medium-sized are at least able to send selected Africans for further training in the United States, and the smallest companies do not have the resources to do either. However, the speed with which Africanization reaches the upper managerial positions reverses this order, with the smallest companies first. It is said that the smaller companies are the ones which are best able to teach the skills of managerial entrepreneurship, and that in the largest companies the prospects for Africanization do not extend much beyond the supervisory level. But when it comes to the acceptability of Africanization (to the expatriate) the situation is exactly the opposite. In the smallest companies there is the greatest opposition to Africanization, since this is where the expatriate has the most to lose. Furthermore, small companies lack not only the time and money but usually the competence to train Africans, especially in the basic business skills. In the large companies the African is often dissatisfied, especially at being asked to do quasi-manual work in the early training periods; he feels he should belong to a white-collar élite.

Making the dichotomy of direct recruitment from the outside or advancement through the ranks, there is a preference among foreign companies for advancing personnel through the ranks, rather than recruiting directly from outside for higher levels—except for such professionals as the company lawyer or members of the board. Advancement through the ranks may come to trusted older employees or to younger graduates recruited under newer systematic programs. Direct hiring at higher levels will be done in an informal manner through friends or business contacts. Older men who have come up through the ranks are regarded as more reliable and loyal, but on the other hand they may have a lower ultimate ceiling than younger graduates since it is more difficult for them to break the habitual pattern of relationships formed with expatriates many years ago. With the younger men, speed of promotion is a problem: if they are promoted too fast, they may fail and be fired; if promotion comes too slowly, the company will lose them. And, if they are fired, the company may have made a lifetime enemy who may subsequently gain political power.

The concern with middle and top management in this paper neglects a problem pointed out by Hunter.[23] There must be a center layer of men, around the supervisory level, who are capable of intelligently *taking* orders from managers. If not, there is danger that a group of Africans in managerial positions will be giving orders to men below them which are not really understood and which cannot be executed. A lot of supervisory

[23] *Op. cit.*, p. 264.

talent is wasted through lack of training in the most basic skills. And, if managers are being promoted through the ranks, it is important to keep the obvious fact in mind that whenever an African is moved up, it is advisable to have an African to replace him (for example at the supervisory level). Otherwise the whole process of Africanization defeats itself.

Africans may leave the company for the government, and many companies become bitter at the training expense they have invested in a man. But, if the training was good, the company can draw some consolation from knowing that there is a competent man in the government who is familiar with the company's problems. Notably in West Africa, the dropout rate from company training programs is decreasing as a result of better procedures and selection. Politically, foreign companies just cannot afford to discontinue their training programs.

Moreover, the situation has recently begun to take on an interesting new dimension. As the romance of government work begins to wear off and bureaucracy begins to chafe, the African may come back into private business—which has meanwhile adjusted itself better to having Africans in positions of authority. As a result, there is increasing movement between business and government, and the resulting dialogue and mutual understanding can do only good for the company's long-run prospects.

Conflicting affiliations. An appreciation of the African socio-political structure is of great importance. A man not only has a place in the company hierarchy but usually a place (and concomitant responsibilities) in the tribal or communal hierarchy. (This is quite unlike the usual case in the United States, where the social reference group tends to progress with movement within the company structure.) As a result, a conflict can arise when a man's company standing is higher than that of someone whose communal or tribal standing is higher. Likewise, political affiliation can be more important than in the United States, especially since political divisions often parallel tribal lines.

Moreover, ambivalent attitudes can occur between Africans of different nationalities—an important point for a multi-country company which wants to move Africans within its African operations to gain experience. Someone reporting to an African of different nationality may ask himself, "If Africans are good enough for this position, why not me?" The continued acceptance of an expatriate as someone who is eligible for a higher position also is reflected here. Furthermore, the position cannot now be gotten by the subordinate on the basis of Africanization: an African now has it.

Incidentally, it does not appear that American Negroes are especially successful in African operations on the basis of race alone.

Salary differentials. Lastly we come to the problem of salary differentials. Unfortunately, the question of international executive compensation is not economically rational. As a rule, an expatriate will get a significantly higher salary than an African in the same job, this being especially true in American as against European companies.

The area of compensation is the most sensitive to comparisons on the basis of fairness and equality, and in the process of Africanization it is the African who is likely to feel badly treated. In the process of transition there is also the probability that an African will have an expatriate subordinate who is receiving a higher salary, a condition which is not conducive to organizational harmony.

4. THE CRUCIAL PROBLEM: PERSONAL ATTITUDES

"No matter what the abilities of the African, his expatriate superior will not give a good report."—Tanzanian Civil Servant Concerned with Private-Sector Africanization.

"The young Africans hired as prospective management material have an unrealistic expectation of how quickly they will be promoted."—Oil Company Executive

Undeniably, "Africanization" has emotional connotations to the participants. Historically, white skin became synonymous with foreign oppression and ill-treatment; black skin came to be looked on as a mark of inferiority. Advances in sociology and psychology have eradicated these crude notions intellectually on both sides but emotional reactions die a slower death. This is most definitely not to claim that all the problems of Africanization can be traced to a common cause, but to wear blinkers in the face of the problem would be equally mistaken.

Recently Mr. Mboya warned foreign businesses to Africanize their operations in Kenya or face government take-over.[24] He said: "The Government cannot accept that businesses in the main streets of our urban areas will continue to be owned exclusively by non-Africans, nor would it be right for [such] a situation to prevail in a predominantly African country." If Africanization is not undertaken, "the Government will face enormous pressures for drastic action." That he said "owned" rather than "run" is of less importance than the principle involved, which is that of who shall visibly wield power. The pressure is on moderate governments to preempt extremist criticism, and reducing foreign influence in an African

24 *The New York Times,* May 6, 1966, p. 12.

country is a little more clear-cut than in France: A black man behind the desk makes the point. In an address to the Zambian Institute of Management Dr. Kaunda referred to the "razor's edge" he was having to tread in balancing the claims for rapid Africanization against the maintenance of reasonable industrial efficiency.[25]

There is no doubt that as the more moderate politicians become convinced that suitable Africans exist, they will put a great deal of pressure on foreign companies. The country belongs to Africans now, and the manifestly white skins of those wielding economic power are an affront; nations want to be the masters of their own destiny. "Most of Nigeria's economic difficulties can only be solved when foreign business concerns operating in Nigeria are in the hands of Nigerian businessmen . . . until then all talk of economic progress will be useless."[26]

The issue is emotional indeed, and not only racial but nationalistic as well: The process of Africanization is referred to not only as such but also as Kenyanization, Nigerianization, and so on. Psychologically, African countries may be said to be fighting for recognition on their own terms, as being what they are, and not the white man's black sheep. There is an increasing sense of a historically unique identity. "Because of the myth that the African has no culture and no history, colonial policies—political, social, and economic—are all directed to the transformation of the African into an inferior white man. [But] when the medieval universities . . . were flourishing in Europe, the twelfth-century University of Sankore . . . was an established center of West African enlightenment."[27]

This is the background for the continually repeated view on the African side that foreign companies are not promoting Africans as quickly as they should. The continued and visible absence of Africans in responsible positions aggravates both the pressures and the suspicions. Now, there *are* factually well-founded reports of seeming lack of competence on the part of Africans when given responsibility. This would seem to have two bases: one cultural, the other inherent in the psychological structure of the situation.

Few of the institutions and values of traditional African society lay a groundwork for the motivations, attitudes, and restraints which are re-

---

[25] ILO Survey No. 4. See Note 12.

[26] Waziri Ibrahim, Minister of Economic Development, reported in *West Africa*, April 11, 1964 (quoted in Proehl, *op. cit.*, p. 172).

[27] Dike, K. Onwuka, "History and African Nationalism," in *Proceedings of the Annual Conference of the West African Institute of Social and Economic Research*, Ibadan, 1952.

quired of a man to make a success in a foreign company. The Protestant Ethic, the drive to hard work and achievement as an end in itself, on which Western industrial society was largely built, is absent in Africa. Basic mechanical manipulative skills, in the form of toys, do not help to shape the life of the average African child; neither is he exposed to the day-to-day talk about business matters which is usual in the United States (with the consequent absorption of attitudes and values). As a result, so many of the presuppositions about life which are taken for granted by expatriates are not present in the African. Thus there is a much greater need to give full instructions and to explain what exactly is expected of a man when he is given certain responsibilities.

The tendency among some African groups to be overly polite, too embarrassed to question foreigners further when they do not understand a point, adds to the difficulties. But to explain failure in terms of innate stupidity or laziness instead of problems of cultural adaptation makes matters much worse. A policy based on presumed lack of innate endowment will set up a psychological situation where the African is likely to react as if this were actually the case, and the expatriate will be reinforced in his mistaken behavioral pattern. Given a basic competence and some cultural empathy, there is little reason to believe that the Western dictum, "Give a man responsibility, show him that you trust him, and he will do a good job," does not apply to Africans.

An American who has had experience in training Africans in sophisticated business techniques points out three areas where many expatriates make a fundamental error in their approach:

1. *Selection of candidates*. There is an absence of advanced selection techniques, with too much reliance on simply advertising and then interviewing.
2. *Learning requirements*. Africans are generally anxious to educate themselves further, but in the process they may not perform as well as they could because teaching techniques are not related to the African environment and its requirements.
3. *Estimates of ability*. The abilities of the African are often grossly underestimated, as to both mental capabilities and staying power.

This American has found that under proper conditions, the clichés regarding Africans' deficiencies are shown to be erroneous, but that the problem of the application of theory to practice is the main area where adjustments have to be made in teaching techniques.

Very clearly, it is extremely advantageous to send African employees to the United States to be fully exposed to the system in which they will have to work. An awareness of the role of experience as opposed to just "learning" how to be a manager may also be promoted in this way. Among eager Africans the dictum is: "Teach us how to manage, and we shall be good managers"; formal education and training are almost overvalued—to the detriment of the need for experience (a phenomenon also observed among youth in the West). As a result, there is what seems to be unrealistic impatience among African employees and government officials regarding a man's promotional capabilities and, consequently, suspicion that the African is being unfairly held back.

In some cases it is undoubtedly true that the African is indeed being unfairly held back, usually because of conscious or unconscious job protection by his expatriate superior. Shearer[28] describes this cycle for Latin America, where localization has gone much further. There is a naive belief that localization will occur "naturally" as the investment matures, but expatriate job protection is inherent in the structure of most companies and therefore expatriates "cannot find" nationals. Those who are developed are handled ineptly so that when a vacancy occurs they are "not qualified" to fill it and a request will be sent for another American. Then, when the American is installed, the whole cycle repeats itself. Shearer recommends that the home office refuse to send any more personnel on a career basis, so that the subsidiary will be forced to develop nationals. He observes that in establishing their judgmental criteria, expatriate managers seem to demand perfection from a national before promoting him, whereas they are more tolerant toward other Americans. As a result, there is never a national around who can "handle the job." This also affects the type of national who will work for the company; "the very nationals with the greatest promise are those most likely to be repelled by the low ceiling on opportunities and the various forms of discrimination which are the usual consequences of American domination." In this way a vicious circle is perpetuated.

The crucial problem indicated by job protection is that of providing assurances for the expatriate who has to bring an African into his own position, and this may not always be easy for the company. But unless the expatriate can feel reassured, he will be wise in keeping down a promising African. This problem is likely to increase as Africanization moves up the management ladder. At present, mainly low and middle management positions are being Africanized, and expatriates have a greater number of posts to move up into.

[28] *Op. cit.,* p. 129.

The personnel manager of a large U.S. company operating in many African countries describes his main problem as that of getting the type of expatriate who will recognize and take the most talented African as an understudy, bring him along as quickly as possible, and step aside for him at the earliest opportunity. His problem is that every expatriate invariably sees himself at the topmost level of ability and most Africans near the bottom, with other expatriates somewhere in the middle. Since the expatriate himself will probably be somewhere in the middle of the ability range, he instinctively picks an African well below that level, so as to maintain his own self-esteem. Even the most "liberal" expatriate will pick a "just educated" African with the attitude that, "Well, here is an African who can actually *do* something!" The ideal but elusive expatriate is one who has a lot of ability and is able to train, as an equal, an African who he recognizes to have just as much ability as he himself has, if not more.

Old-fashioned snobbery and prejudice are of course not entirely absent. For example, in one area dominated by a foreign company some communities are made up of 45 percent South African whites, combined with British expatriates of gentlemanly heritage. As a result, most Africans are socially unacceptable unless they have studied at Oxbridge. It has been virtually impossible to promote an African into a responsible position because he would need a secretary, and the only secretaries available have been whites who refuse to work under an African. But often the problems are class- rather than race-oriented as the élite Africans absorb class attitudes and move in expatriate circles socially. And social exclusivity, whether by a group of expatriates alone or a group of expatriate and African managers together, can only foster an adverse image for the company.

"No American company would dream of stating publicly, especially in the host country, that the services of the best nationals it could employ are worth but a fraction of those second-string Americans it has seen fit to import, and yet their actions testify to this conviction."[29] Economically, a man's salary reflects what he is worth to the company; therefore, if it was worthwhile to have an American at $20,000 per year, an African doing the same job is also worth $20,000. The principle of the same pay for the same job as between men and women has gained some acceptance in the West, and the case for the African manager rests on the same foundations. However, many noneconomic factors have modified this situation, and in fact an African manager can expect very much less than his American equal. The argument goes that if one man is paid on the

[29] Shearer, *op. cit.,* p. 133.

American scale, everyone will want similar treatment. This clearly has a lot of validity. The result is of course beneficial in terms of speeding the Africanization process, but in some cases it may have been overdone.

Some observers point out that often the salaries they have found American companies offering Africans are ridiculously low, driving away all but the most marginally competent. This also is a form of job protection, but in practicing it companies only perpetuate their problems in not getting good Africans, becoming more firmly convinced that Africans are not worth high salaries. Generally, too, the standing of business, and a career in it, remains low. It is notable that a business career in India became increasingly acceptable for more able men as the salary levels rose.[30]

A Tanzanian official describes how he carefully and circumspectly approaches a foreign company to avoid upsetting management when he calls to inquire how its Africanization program is coming along; in pursuing Zambianization, the Zambian Government is concerned lest it cause too much uncertainty among foreign companies; a foreign personnel manager worries about the type of expatriate he can find to implement Africanization. And so it goes. An understanding of the less rational fears and prejudices of both sides will help immeasurably in smoothing the progress of foreign companies in Africa.

In particular, one may be struck by this paradox: African governments hold the ultimate power over the employment of expatriates through the granting of working permits, and they adhere to the principle that if there is a qualified African, he must have the job. Yet they complain that Africanization and qualified Africans are being deliberately kept back, and that there are more expatriates around than there should be. One suspects that some power-based bargains are being struck behind the scenes. But another factor may also be present, one that is encouraging for American companies: they are dealing with reasonable men who appreciate the value of foreign capital and its judgment of a man's capabilities. Yet these reasonable men also have a domestic political arena where they want to survive, and they must therefore proclaim the need for greater Africanization. It is not that they don't believe in what they say; the tempo of Africanization *must* quicken as more Africans are able to take on managerial jobs. Otherwise increasing pressures will be brought to bear, maybe after the moderates have been ousted by others less patient.

[30] ILO Survey No. 4, *op. cit.*, p. 11.